TIME FOR KIDS

SUPER SCIENCE BOOK

Get a grown-up's permission and help with the experiments!

POWERED BY Mad SCIENCE®

Lynnette Brent Sandvold

Time Home Entertainment
Publisher: Richard Fraiman
General Manager: Steven Sandonato
Executive Director, Marketing Services: Carol Pittard
Director, Retail & Special Sales: Tom Mifsud
Director, New Product Development: Peter Harper
Director, Bookazine Development & Marketing: Laura Adam
Publishing Director: Joy Butts
Assistant General Counsel: Helen Wan
Design & Prepress Manager: Anne-Michelle Gallero
Book Production Manager: Susan Chodakiewicz
Associate Brand Manager: Jonathan White
Associate Prepress Manager: Alex Voznesenskiy

TIME For Kids
Managing Editor, TIME For Kids Magazine: Nellie Gonzalez Cutler
Editor, TIME Learning Ventures: Jonathan Rosenbloom

Created by **Q2AMedia**
Publishing Director: Chester Fisher
Editor: Penny Dowdy
Art Director: Rahul Dhiman
Senior Designer: Harleen Mehta
Designers: Neha Kaul, Ritu Chopra
Picture Researcher: Sanjay Rawat
Illustrators: Ashish Tanwar, Danish Zaidi, Indranil Ganguly, Madhavi Poddar, Nazia Zaidi, Rohit Sharma, Vinay Kumar Sharma

Special Thanks to:
Alexandra Bliss, Glenn Buonocore, Christine Font, Lauren Hall, Suzanne Janso, Malena Jones, Robert Marasco, Kimberly Marshall, Amy Migliaccio, Shelley Rescober, Nina Mistry, Ilene Schreider, Adriana Tierno, Vanessa Wu

Published by TIME For Kids Books, an imprint of Time Home Entertainment Inc.
135 West 50th Street
New York, New York 10020

ISBN 13: 978-1-60320-812-3
ISBN 10: 1-60320-812-7

3 QGT 11

We welcome your comments and suggestions about TIME For Kids Books.
Please write to us at:
TIME For Kids Books
Attention: Book Editors
PO Box 11016
Des Moines, IA 50336-1016

If you would like to order any of our hardcover Collector's Edition books, please call us at 1-800-327-6388. (Monday through Friday, 7:00 a.m.— 8:00 p.m. or Saturday, 7:00 a.m.— 6:00 p.m. Central Time).

Picture credits
t=top b=bottom c=centre l=left r=right

Cover Image: NASA: tl, Bychkov Kirill Alexandrovich/ Shutterstock: tr, Jupiterimages: bl

Back Cover Image: PeopleStockPhotography

Benedek/ Istockphoto: 6, Comstock Images/ Jupiterimages: 7, Fayaz Kabli/ Reuters: 8t, Jeff Barnard/ Apimages: 8b, Paul Zoller/ Apimages: 9t, Radu Razvan/ Shutterstock: 9b, Giovanni Benintende/ Shutterstock: 10t, Shutterstock: 10b, Rebecca Hale/ NG: 11t, Marmion/ Bigstockphoto: 11b, Natalia Bratslavsky/ Istockphoto: 12t, ileximage/ Istockphoto: 12b, Lugo Graphics/ Istockphoto: 13t, Henri S. Faure/ Istockphoto: 13b, Morgan Lane/ Shutterstock: 14tl, Interact Publishing/ Istockphoto: 14tr, Kay Burn Lim/ Dreamstime: 15, Andrea Danti/ Dreamstime: 16t, Bram Janssens/ Dreamstime; 16b, Shevelev Vladimir/ Dreamstime, Fallsview/ Dreamstime, Dianne McFadden/ Shutterstock: 18tl, Bronwyn/ Istockphoto: 18tr, Julien Grondin/ Istockphoto: 18b, Hauserworks/ Istockphoto: 19, NickS/ Istockphoto: 20r, NOOA Photolibrary: 20c, Marilyn Barbone/ 123rf: 20l, Sandra Henderson/ Dreamstime: 21, Tim Boyle/ Gettyimages: 21t, Jeffrey L. Rotman/ Corbis: 21lb, Arpad Benedek/ Istockphoto: 21rb, kjscrafts/ Bigstockphoto: 23, Michael Lynch/ Dreamstime: 24tr, Elena Elisseeva/ Shutterstock: 24tl, Istockphoto: 24b, Marti Comas/ Fotolia: 26t, Dreamstime: 26b, JulienGrondin/ Dreamstime: 28, Mike Dunning/ Gettyimages: 30t, Lee Prince/ Shutterstock: 30b, Stillfx/ Shutterstock:32t, Vulnifican/ Stockxpert: 32bl, Martin Horsky/ Shutterstock:32br, Dreamstime: 33, Stockxpert: 34, Alexander Shalamov/ Shutterstock: 36, Marilyn Barbone/ Shutterstock, Ron Chapple Studios/ Dreamstime, Kris Butler/ Shutterstock, Sanjay Rawat/ Q2AMedia:37t, Mike Derer/ Apimages: 37b, Ted Soqui/ Corbis: 40tl, Lori Mehmen/ Apimages: 40tr, Peter Kirschner/ 123rf: 42, Tad Denson/ Shutterstock: 43t, Caltech/ NASA and JPL: 43b, Molly Riley/ Reuters: 45, George Nazmi Bebawi/ Shutterstock: 46t, Mark Baskett/ 123rf: 46b, NOOA Photolibrary: 47, Emin Kuliyev/ Shutterstock: 48t, Tischenko Irina/ Shutterstock: 48bl, Amridesign/ Istockphoto: 48br, Oliver Hoffmann/ Shutterstock: 49t, Tom Hirtreiter/ Shutterstock: 49b, Eril Nisbett/ Dreamstime: 50t, Laurent Dambies/ Shutterstock: 50b, Dave Wetzel/ Shutterstock: 52t, Nobor/ Shutterstock: 52b, Ariel Bravy/ Shutterstock: 53, Cardiae/ Shutterstock: 54tl, SerhioGrey/ Shutterstock: 54tr, Demarcomedia/ Shutterstock: 54b, Joseph Helfenberger/ Dreamstime: 54bg, Willem Dijkstra/ Shutterstock: 56t, David Iushewitz/ Dreamstime: 56b, Pritz Franz/ Alamy: 60tr, Corbis: 60cl, Anton J Geisser: 60br, Bigstockphoto: 62, Canstockphoto: 66, Istockphoto: 68, Vilmos Varga/ Shutterstock: 70t, Griffin/ Bigstockphoto: 70b, Paul A. Souders/ Corbis: 72tr, Bigstockphoto: 72tc, lantapix/ Bigstockphoto: 72b, Istockphoto: 74t, Ian Bracegirdle/ Dreamstime: 74b, Alex Staroseltsev/ Shutterstock: 74c, Scott Griessel/ Dreamstime: 76bl, Tomas Loutocky/ Dreamstime: 78tr, Shutterstock, Istockphoto: 78cr, Christina Richards/ Dreamstime: 78bl, Olivier Le Queinec/ Shutterstock, Dmitry Rukhlenko/ Shutterstock: 78cb, Alvin Teo/ Dreamstime: 78br, Hongqi Zhang/ Dreamstime: 80t, Shutterstock: 80b, Carolina K. Smith/ Shutterstock: 82t, Richard Lindie/ Dreamstime: 82b, Naluphoto/ Shutterstock: 83t, Monkey Business Images/ Shutterstock: 83b, Lena Grottling/ Shutterstock: 84tr, Glenn R. McGloughlin/ Shutterstock: 84c, Eric Isselée/ Shutterstock: 84cr, Mighty Sequoia Studio/ Shutterstock: 84bl, Morozova Tatyana/ Shutterstock: 84br, CathyKeifer/ Bigstockphoto: 86t, Photolibrary/ Robin Smith: 86b, Phil/ Dreamstime: 88t, BeholdingEye/ Istockphoto: 88b, Jerry Zitterman/ Shutterstock: 90t, Canstockphoto; 90b, Liv friis-larsen/ Shutterstock: 92, Oguz Aral/ Shutterstock: 94t, Martin Bangemann/ Shutterstock: 94b, Iris Schneider/ Dreamstime: 96, Sebastian Kaulitzki/ Shutterstock: 98c, Basov Mikhail/ Shutterstock: 98r, Lisa F. Young/ Shutterstock: 100t, Lucwa/ Shutterstock, Sviecia/ Shutterstock, Anthony Harris/ Dreamstime: 100c, Cre8tive Images/ Shutterstock: 100b, Oleg Seleznev/ Fotolia: 102t, Shutterstock, Enia/ Shutterstock: 102c, Galyna Andrushko: 102b, Drimi/ 123rf: 103, Stuart Hepburn/ 123rf: 104t, Dgphotography/ Bigstockphoto: 104b, Filev/ Stockxpert: 106t, Veronika Vasilyuk/ Shutterstock: 106b, Geza Farkas/ Dreamstime: 107, Vera Jordanova/ Dreamstime: 108t, Shutterstock: 108b, HP_photo/ Shutterstock: 110c, mylifeiscamp/ Shutterstock: 110tr, MPI/ Stringer/ Hulton Archive/ Gettyimages: 110b, Mario Lopes/ Shutterstock: 112t, Juan Manuel Ordóñez/ Shutterstock: 112b, Jacek Chabraszewski/ Shutterstock: 113, Letty/ 123rf: 114, Peter Cade/ Gettyimages: 115t, BartCo/ Istockphoto: 115b, Rob Marmion/ Shutterstock: 116bl, Rob Marmion/ Shutterstock: 116br, Anyka/ Shutterstock: 117

CONTENTS

THINK LIKE A SCIENTIST

Who Are Scientists? What Do They Do?

This paleontologist checks out a huge fossil.

Paleontologists dig up the remains of organisms that lived long ago. **Geologists** study rocks to find out more about the Earth. **Entomologists** study insects. What do all these people have in common? They are just a few of the many types of scientists. Scientists observe, study, look for patterns, and try to find general rules to explain how things work. Scientists might study **volcanoes**, simple machines, and animals that live deep under the ocean. Understanding these rules often helps scientists create or improve processes that we use in our world every day. Scientists look for **laws** that explain how or why things happen. A scientific law describes something that has been observed many times. Scientists can use a law to predict what will happen. The laws of **gravity**, for example, explain why we stick to the Earth instead of floating away. Police use laws of motion to understand what happened at a traffic accident.

The Scientific Method

Scientists look for facts that explain the world around us.

Scientists follow a set of steps. We call this process the **scientific method**. The scientific method is a path that scientists can follow to keep their work organized. It also helps them to look for science-based answers to problems or questions.

What happens in the scientific method? Scientists make observations that lead to generalizations about why some event happens. These "first guess" generalizations are called hypotheses.

One successful event might just be an accident or a fluke. Scientists test a **hypothesis** many times to make sure it wasn't something that happens just one time. A good experiment shows something can happen again and again. The scientist experiments to look for facts that explain what they observe. As scientists test a hypothesis and continue to observe, they look for **evidence** to support the hypothesis. If they can support the hypothesis, it may lead to a **theory** or a law of science.

All scientists use six basic skills in the scientific method: observing, communicating, classifying, measuring, inferring, and predicting. You've read about a few of them already. Let's look at each one.

Observing

We notice things around us. The gray **clouds** coming in from the west warn of a coming storm. The steam rising from the hot cocoa tells us to sip carefully. The sirens in the distance let us know to move out of the way for a fire truck.

Scientists observe, too. We all use our **senses** to get information about the world around us. We can use tools to observe, too, such as microscopes, magnifying glasses, and telescopes in space. Scientists do not include opinions in their observations. They only record what they observe.

Scientists observe and take careful notes.

Communicating

Scientists share their observations.

When scientists make new discoveries, they share them. Communicating is a way to share observations, discoveries, and results. Scientists communicate their results in many ways. They write or draw. They use visual aids such as graphs, charts, maps, diagrams, and multimedia presentations. When you do science experiments, be sure that your communication is clear and direct. Your audience should understand what happened.

Classifying

Classifying objects is grouping them according to how they are similar, how they are different, or how they are related to each other. In the classroom, a teacher might have students line up in alphabetical order. That's one simple way to classify. Scientists classify everything from animals to planets.

What kind of rocks are these? The geologists classify them to find out.

Measuring

Scientists also use measuring tools to make precise observations and clear records of what they observe. For example, you can put your hand outside and know that it's hot. But you need a thermometer to know the exact temperature. Other tools **measure** mass, distance, volume, and time.

This scale is a precise measuring tool.

Inferring and Predicting

Inferring means using observations and what you know to figure something out. Scientists infer all the time. Imagine a scientist observing a small insect. Every time a larger insect comes near the small one, the small insect releases a dark, sticky **liquid** from its body. The larger insect flies away. If the scientist saw this many times, she could eventually figure out, or infer, that the liquid helps the small insect defend itself. Then she could predict, too. If another large insect or an animal comes near the smaller insect, the smaller insect should release the liquid again.

Branches of Science

There are many branches, or areas of study, in science. Here are just a few:

- *astronomy:* the study of celestial objects in the universe
- *biology:* the study of living organisms
- *botany:* the study of plant life
- *ecology:* the study of how organisms interact with each other and their environment
- *genetics:* the study of heredity
- *meteorology:* the study of the atmosphere that focuses on weather processes and forecasting
- *physics:* the study of the behavior and properties of matter
- *thermodynamics:* the physics of energy, heat, and work

Mireya Mayor is a scientist and an explorer. On a special trip to Madagascar she found a new animal species, a tiny animal called a mouse lemur. Her discovery had an important effect. The prime minister of Madagascar decided to turn the place where these animals live into a national park. Now the animals can live safely, and scientists can study the newly-discovered species. Scientists can have amazing effects on the world!

Mireya Mayor is a National Geographic Emerging Explorer.

Play It Safe!

Wear goggles to protect your eyes.

You'll find some interesting and fun projects in this book. Remember to be safe when you do these projects. These rules will keep you safe in the kitchen, backyard, lab, or wherever else you do science:

- Be sure safety equipment is nearby. If you are doing an experiment with heat, know where you can find a fire extinguisher.
- If you are going to handle something hot, you need to use potholders or thick gloves.
- Read all the instructions before you begin. Ask an adult to help you with steps you don't understand.
- Do not eat or drink any parts of an experiment unless you are told to.
- Pull back long hair so it's out of the way.
- Be sure you clean up all surfaces when you're done with experiments.
- Wear shoes with closed toes when you are doing experiments.
- Get adult help with anything sharp, electric, or hot.

WHAT IS EARTH SCIENCE?

What makes a **hurricane** form over the ocean? How do we get petroleum from the Earth—and how long will Earth's supply last? Which are the biggest lakes? What rocks and minerals are valuable, and why? Where in the **solar system** is Earth?

How did that tiny river help carve this massive canyon?

Wind blows sand into dunes—strange and beautiful desert features.

All these questions are part of a branch of science called **earth science**. Earth science studies the composition, formation, and structure of our planet Earth. In this part of the book, you'll find out more about the Earth, from volcanoes and **fossils** to weather and seasons. You'll find out how to make a gauge to collect rainwater, model the solar system, and make a volcano explode right in your own kitchen. The activities in this section invite you to learn more about our wonderful planet, Earth!

Lightning is nature's electricity.

Volcanoes are dramatic features of Earth.

Amazing Science!

The Sun looks yellow to our eyes here on Earth, but if you looked at it from outer space or from the surface of the Moon, it would appear white.

EARTH
Is It Really a Giant Magnet?

What does a refrigerator magnet have in common with our planet, Earth? Believe it or not, they're both magnets.

The pieces of metal show us the magnetic field.

MAGNETS

A **magnet** is a material that **attracts** iron and iron compounds with a **force** called **magnetism**. Steel can become a magnet itself when stroked against naturally magnetic iron ores called lodestones. Magnetic force can pull metal objects toward the magnet and sometimes even push them away. It's strong enough that a small refrigerator magnet can hold papers on your refrigerator. Magnets create areas of space around them called **magnetic fields**. The magnetic field becomes weaker at a distance.

Just like all magnets, Earth has a magnetic field around it. You cannot see Earth's magnetic field. But it is all around you.

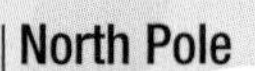

South Pole

A PAIR OF POLES

Magnets have two poles. A pole is another name for the end of a magnet. One pole is called the north pole. The other is the south pole. The magnetic force is strongest at a magnet's poles. Where else do you use the terms north and south pole? Exactly—when talking about our planet. Earth has a north pole and a south pole , although Earth's magnetic poles and geographic poles to match exactly.. In magnets, like poles **repel** and opposites attract. You can try this with small magnets. If you put the south poles of two magnets near each other, they won't stick together. In fact, the magnetic force will push them apart.

Magnetic Fields

It probably would be difficult for you to measure the magnetic field all around Earth. However, you can use simple materials to observe a magnetic field.

You will need:

- box of uncoated paper clips
- bar magnet with the north (N) and south (S) poles

1

Make a pile of paper clips on a table.

2

Touch the south pole of the magnet to the paper clips. Lift up the magnet. What happens?

3 Touch the north pole of the magnet to the paper clips. Lift up the magnet. What happens?

4 Touch the side of the magnet to the paper clips. Lift up the magnet. What happens?

THE SCIENCE BEHIND IT!

A magnet is a special **metal**. **Magnets** attract things made of steel or iron, like paper clips. Magnets have north and south poles with space between them. A **magnetic field** is like a big bubble around a magnet. It starts at the magnet's north pole and loops around to the south pole. The magnet is strongest at its poles. The magnet attracted the paper clips when you touched its poles, the ends of the magnet, to the pile. The attracted paper clips form a loop when you dip the side of the magnet into the pile. This loop shows what the magnetic field looks like.

Animal Magnetism

Scientists believe many animals are influenced by Earth's magnetic field. Some scientists are studying migrating birds. The scientists want to know if Earth's magnetic field guides the birds in the direction they travel. Other scientists are studying to see if sea turtles feel the influence of Earth's magnetic field as they swim across the ocean.

Where in the SOLAR SYSTEM Is Earth?

Sun

Mercury

Earth

Venus

Mars

Jupiter

Saturn

Uranus

Neptune

You probably know your neighborhood pretty well. You know how to get from home to school and back. You probably know a great place to meet your friends to play. But how well do you know Earth's neighborhood?

THIRD ROCK FROM THE SUN

Earth is the third planet from the Sun. But Earth is much different from all the other planets. It is the only planet known to have living things. Earth has just the right "ingredients" for life to exist. Its average temperature is 59° F, (15° C), it has plenty of water, and it is surrounded by just the right type of **atmosphere** to support life. Earth certainly is home sweet home!

This is the view of Earth from space.

OUR SOLAR SYSTEM

The Sun is the center of our **solar system**. A solar system is a group of planets that revolves around one common star. Our Sun is a star. There are eight planets in our solar system. Mercury, Venus, Earth, and Mars are the planets closest to the Sun. This group is also called the **rocky planets**: these planets are made mostly of rock. Jupiter, Saturn, Uranus, and Neptune are the next four planets. These planets are sometimes called the **gas** giants: *giants* because they are much bigger in size than the other planets, and *gas* because those planets are made mostly of gasses. Pluto was once classified as a planet, but scientists today don't consider Pluto a planet. Some believe that Pluto is too small to be considered a planet. It's only as big as a average-sized moon.

Model the Solar System

How far apart are the planets? You'd be amazed at the distances.

- cardstock paper (5 sheets)
- colored pencils
- flashlight
- compass
- scissors
- black marker
- 7 ft (2.1 m) kite string
- measuring tape
- hole punch
- 2 chairs

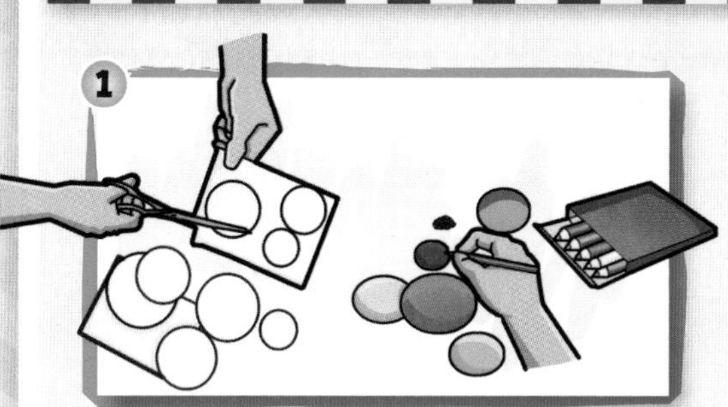

1. Use the chart below to create paper circles for each planet. Write the planets' names on the circles. For the asteroid belt, cut a 2-inch square and color it brown and grey.

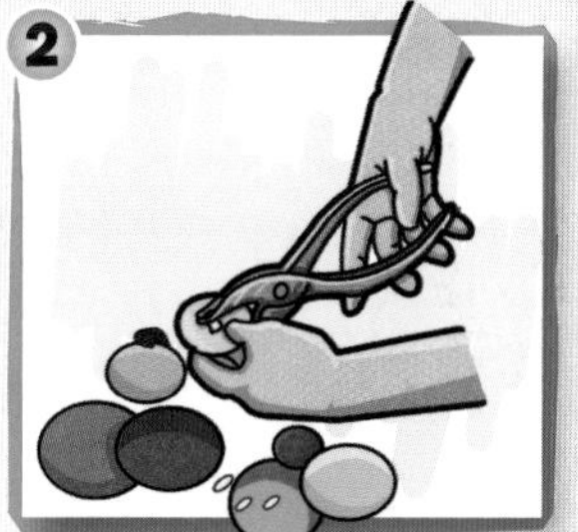

2. Punch a small hole in the center of each circle.

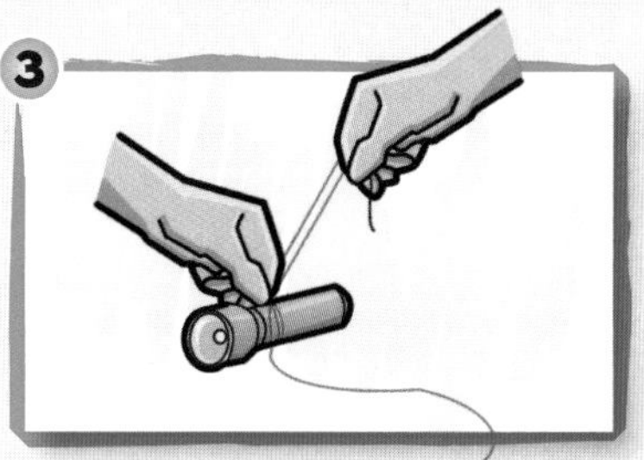

3. Tie a knot about 6 in. (15 cm) from one end of the string. This knot is where your Sun will be. Tie your flashlight to this spot.

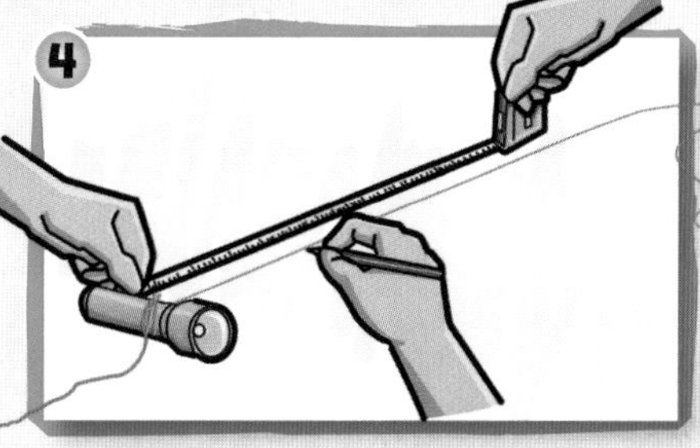

4. Use the measures on the chart to mark the string at each planet's distance.

5. Thread the string through the center hole of each planet. Slide each planet to the correct mark on the string.

6. Tie the ends of the string to two chairs. Separate the chairs until the string is tight. Turn on the flashlight.

THE SCIENCE BEHIND IT!

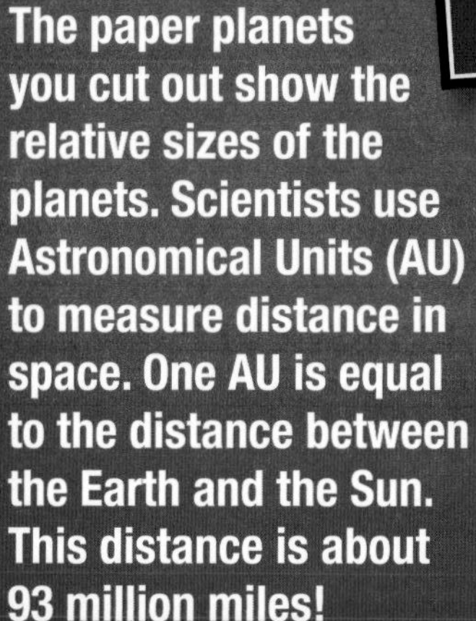

The paper planets you cut out show the relative sizes of the planets. Scientists use Astronomical Units (AU) to measure distance in space. One AU is equal to the distance between the Earth and the Sun. This distance is about 93 million miles!

Planet	Color	Planet Diameter	Distance from the Sun	Distance in AU*
Mercury	red	0.7 in. (1.8 cm)	1.0 in. (2.5 cm)	0.4
Venus	beige	1.9 in. (4.8 cm)	1 3/4 in. (4.4 cm)	0.7
Earth	blue and green	2.0 in. (5.1 cm)	2 1/2 in. (6.4 cm)	1.0
Mars	red	1.0 in. (2.5 cm)	3 3/4 in. (9.5 cm)	1.5
Asteroid belt	black	-	7.0 in. (17.8 cm)	2.8
Jupiter	orange	22.0 in. (55.9 cm)	12 1/2 in. (31.8 cm)	5.0
Saturn	gold	18.5 in. (47.0 cm)	25.0 in. (63.5 cm)	10.0
Uranus	dark blue	7.9 in. (20.1 cm)	47 1/2 in. (120.7 cm)	19.0
Neptune	light blue	7.6 in. (19.3 cm)	75.0 in. (190.5 cm)	30.0

* Astronomical Units

HARD AS A ROCK:
How Are Rocks Formed?

Granite . . . sandstone . . . shale. What do these names have in common? They are all names of rocks. Rocks fall into three different categories: sedimentary, metamorphic, and igneous (IG nee uhs). They form in different ways and have different properties.

TURN UP THE HEAT

Another name for igneous rock is "fire rock." Why? Some igneous rocks form under heat and pressure deep within the Earth when melted rock, called **magma**, cools. Magma can also ooze or be blown out of volcanoes as lava. Cooled lava creates other kinds of igneous rock.

This hot lava can turn into igneous rock.

Sedimentary rocks form in streams like this.

IT'S SEDIMENTARY!

One kind of rock is just like a layer cake. Sedimentary rock such as sandstone forms when little pieces of earth break down and are worn away by wind and water. These pieces of earth eventually wash downstream. They settle on the bottoms of rivers, lakes, streams , and oceans. Accumulated layers of **sediment** create heat and pressure that turns lower layers into rock.

MORPHING

Metamorphic rocks "morph," or change, from one kind of rock to another. What makes them change? Over long periods of time, heat and pressure changes igneous and sedimentary rocks into metamorphic rocks. Heat and pressure transforms the crystal structure of igneous and sedimentary rock into slate, marble, quartzite and other forms.

Build a Sedimentary Stacker

You can make a model to see how sedimentary rocks form right before your eyes.

You will need:

- 8 oz (237 mL) clear plastic bottle with a cap
- sand
- gravel (or small rocks)
- chalk powder
- water
- paper coffee filter or a funnel
- tablespoon or metric measuring spoon

1

If using a coffee filter, cut a small hole in the bottom of the coffee filter large enough for the gravel to go through.

2

Put the bottom of the coffee filter or the funnel into the opening of the bottle.

3

Add approximately 3-5 tablespoons (44-74 mL) of sand to the bottle.

4

Add approximately 3-5 tablespoons (44-74 mL) of gravel to the bottle.

5

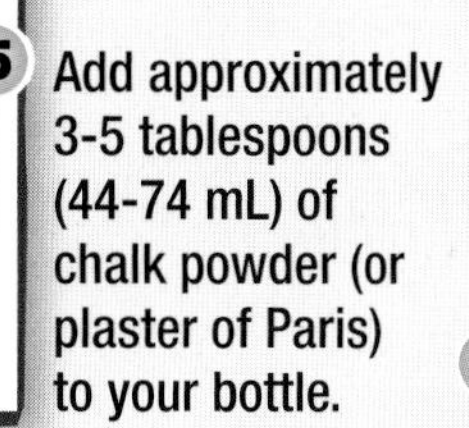

Add approximately 3-5 tablespoons (44-74 mL) of chalk powder (or plaster of Paris) to your bottle.

6

Gently pour water into your bottle so that it is half full. Put the cap on your bottle and shake it to mix the ingredients.

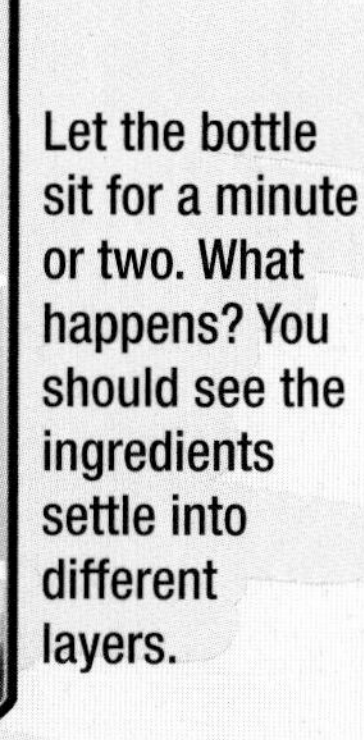

Let the bottle sit for a minute or two. What happens? You should see the ingredients settle into different layers.

Mohs Scale

Talc

Diamond

Some rocks are harder than others, but how can you measure them? In 1812, Frederich Mohs created a scale to rank the hardness of different kinds of rocks. You can compare rocks to the rocks on the scale to classify them. The softest rock on the Mohs scale is talc, ranked 1 on the hardness scale. The hardest rock, with a rank of 10, is diamond.

THE SCIENCE BEHIND IT!

All the materials in the bottle mixed together when you shook it. Then the items assort themselves by particle size. The heaviest sediments, like gravel, fall to the bottom of the bottle. Then different layers form, with the chalk dust ending up at the top. Materials in rivers, lakes, and oceans behave the same way to form sedimentary rocks. Did you notice that the softest powder (with the smallest particle size) made the top layer of sediment? That explains why sand on the surface of some beaches is so soft.

WIND AND WATER

How Do They Shape Earth?

Imagine that you are on top of a mountain. You bend down and pick up a piece of rock, you crumble the rock into smaller pieces, and it blows away. You are now part of a process called erosion.

THE BREAKDOWN

Wind, water, and temperature changes break rock into smaller particles in a process called erosion. Wind, water, and gravity can rearrange these particles into new landforms.

With careful planning, farmers can avoid another erosion disaster.

EROSION IN HISTORY

In the 1930s, wind erosion caused a problem in the southern **Great Plains** in the United States. The plains grew grasses that held the soil in place. Over time, people grew wheat and raised cattle. This exposed the soil to the wind. Scarce rain and heavy winds eroded the soil. In some places four inches (10 cm) of soil was blown away.

The Grand Canyon is a giant example of erosion.

Look at this view of the Grand **Canyon** from an airplane. The Colorado River snakes through the rock. Over time, this great river has dug out a mighty canyon. When rain falls on hard, dry ground, it cannot soak into the soil. Instead, the rain moves fast and breaks up the soil and rocks. The erosion forms canyon walls over millions of years.

Model Erosion

Want to explore erosion? Create a flood in a pan!

You will need:

- 2-3 books
- 1 jelly roll or roasting pan
- soil (moisten it a bit)
- cup
- grass seed (1 tablespoon or 15 mL)
- plastic wrap
- water

1

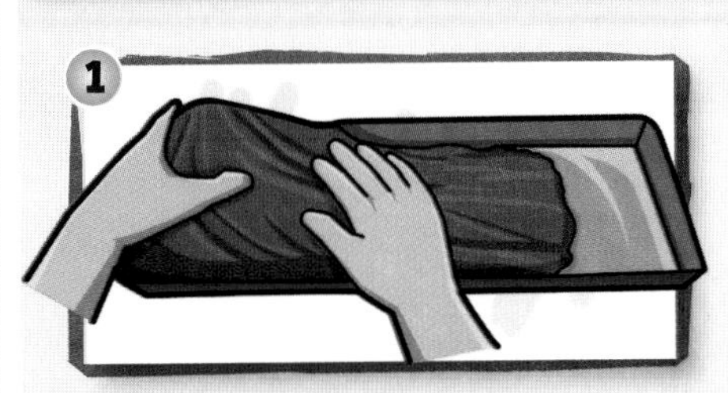

Cover one-half to two-thirds of the pan with moist soil. Gently slope the soil to form a "hill" at one end of the pan.

2

Use the books to lift the end of the pan with the most soil. Fill the cup halfway with water. Carefully pour the water onto the highest part of the pan, forming a river.

3

Sprinkle the grass seed on one side of the river. Cover the pan with plastic wrap and set it in an area with plenty of sunlight. Be sure that the soil in the pan stays moist. Wait about a week, until the grown grass presses against the plastic wrap.

4

Remove the wrap. Use the books to elevate the end of the pan with the most soil in it.

5

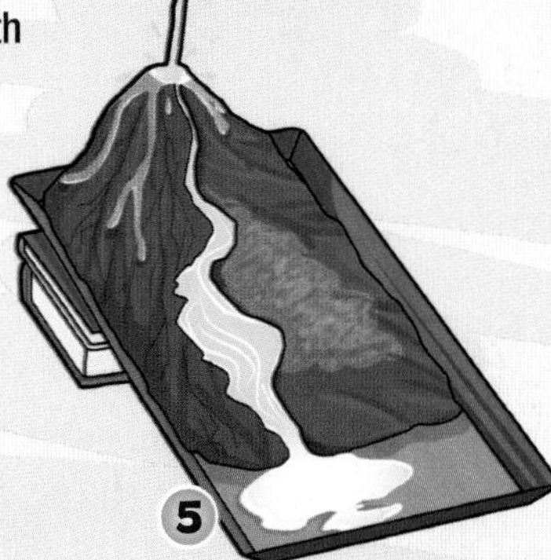

Fill the cup with water. Carefully pour the water into the riverbed. What happens to the soil along the river? Does one side suffer more damage than the other? Why do you think this happens?

In a Flash

Floods are a natural disaster caused by weather. Quick, heavy rainfall combined with hilly terrain creates the recipe for flash floods. Rainwater runs off the steep hillsides into narrow streams. The water level rises rapidly as the streams rush downhill. This raging water can move cars and boulders, uproot trees, and destroy roads, houses, and bridges.

THE SCIENCE BEHIND IT!

Moving water carries soil from one area to another and may destroy crops and farms. The roots of some plants make the soil more resistant to flooding. Planted soil may still suffer damage, though, if there is too much water for it to soak up. When the waters recede, or go back to normal, they leave behind deposits of soil and other debris that can bury or damage plants.

FOSSILS

A Window to Life on Earth

Do you know it's possible to see the types of plants and animals that lived thousands and millions of years ago? It's true—through **fossils.** Fossils are the remains or traces left behind of creatures and plants that once lived on the Earth. They're windows to what life was like during **prehistoric** times.

Fossils help us learn about life long ago.

Living Fossils

Horseshoe crab

Many kinds of plants and animals have lived on Earth. Like dinosaurs, some have died out. Others have changed over time. A few, like the horseshoe crab, exist in a form that has changed little over time. These animals and plants are referred to as living fossils.

HOW FOSSILS FORM

Many fossils form when dead plants and animals are quickly covered by mud or sand, called **sediment**. Sometimes the remains sink to the bottom of a lake or river. The parts of the plant or animal that do not rot, usually the harder parts, are sandwiched in the sediment. A fossil is formed. But not instantly—it may take millions of years.

It's easy to see the leaves of this ancient fern.

Model a Fossil

Some fossils are preserved in a material called amber. Amber is the hardened sap, or resin, of an ancient tree. You can't make a fossil in amber in your kitchen, but you can make a yummy substance that looks like it.

You will need:

- package of yellow or orange gelatin mix
- saucepan with water
- wooden spoon
- paper cup
- edible fossil object (e.g. a nut, dried fruit, or seed)
- adult helper

1. Choose an edible object you want to "fossilize" and put it in a paper cup.

2. Ask your adult helper to prepare the gelatin in the pot on the stove.

3. When it is ready, have your helper pour some liquid gelatin into your cup. Be careful not to touch the hot liquid.

4. Ask your adult helper to put the cup in the fridge, and let it cool there overnight.

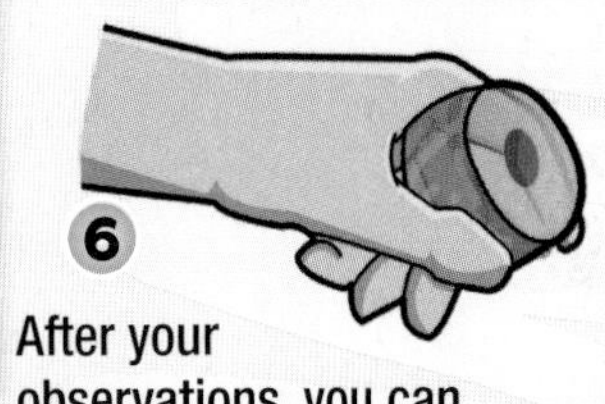

5. The next day, observe your amber-like fossil.

6. After your observations, you can eat your experiment.

A T-Rex Named Sue

Sue is the world's most complete skeleton of a *Tyrannosaurus rex*. She stood over 12 feet (3.7 m) tall from the ground to her hips. She was more than 41 feet (12.5 m) long and had 58 razor-sharp teeth. You can visit Sue at the Field Museum in Chicago.

THE SCIENCE BEHIND IT!

You may have seen amber as a clear, yellow, or orange gem in museums or used in fine jewelry. Amber formed millions of years ago when tree sap seeped from trees and debris such as seeds, leaves, feathers, or insects became trapped in it. As geologic time passed, the trees were buried and the resin hardened. You made a model of preserved fossil remains in amber, but instead of using tree resin, you used gelatin.

THE UPS AND DOWNS IN CAVES

They're homes for animals like brown bats and white eyeless crayfish. You can walk through some of them, and some of them are large enough to hold a tourist boat! What are they? **Caves!** Caves are holes or passages under the earth that occur naturally.

Some bats live in cool, dark caves.

Some caves have spectacular formations!

If You Enter a Cave...

- Never go into a cave by yourself. Always have an adult go with you.
- Ask permission before you enter! Many caves are found in national parks. You can safely enter these caves with guides.
- Tell someone above ground about your plans.
- Bring safety equipment: helmet, first aid kid, three sources of light, water, and food.
- Leave all the natural features as you found them and take out your garbage.

IT STARTS WITH CHEMICALS

Chemistry makes many caves. It starts with simple rainfall. While rain is falling, it absorbs a gas called carbon dioxide from the air around it. Carbon dioxide turns the rainwater into an acid. The acid is weak, but when it falls on certain kinds of rock, the acid can start to eat away at that rock. More and more rock can be worn away. Water flows in and helps erode the rock. Over many thousands or even millions of years, what starts as drips of water in small holes can turn into large holes. Sometimes these large holes become huge systems of holes under the ground.

Make Cave Formations

Stalactites grow down from the ceiling. Stalagmites grow up from the floor. They are both spectacular cave formations!

You will need:

- 2 plastic glasses
- a small plate
- 3 pieces of yarn or string each about 12 inches (30 cm) long
- 2 paperclips
- teaspoon or metric measuring spoon
- baking soda

1 

Fill the two plastic glasses with very warm water. Dissolve as much baking soda in each one as you can.

2 

Place the two plastic glasses in a warm place and put a small plate between them.

3 

Twist or braid three strands of yarn or string together.

4 

Dip one end of the twisted yarn or string in each plastic glass and let it hang down in the middle, over the plate. Clip the twisted string to each glass using a paper clip.

5 Leave the glasses in a warm, dry place for several days. You will see tiny stalactites and stalagmites forming in the middle of the yarn or string and on the plate below it.

Try this: Add some food coloring to your water to create colored formations!

Cave Extremes

- One of the largest stalagmites is in Cuba. It's over 213 feet (65 m) tall!
- Mammoth Cave National Park in Kentucky is home to the largest cave system in the world. Over 335 miles (539 km) of this cave system have been explored and mapped.
- It's hard to know which cave is the deepest. After all, explorers may not have yet reached the bottom. But one of the deepest is Krubera Cave. In 2004, a team of explorers descended 1.2 miles (1.9 km) down into this cave in Russia.

THE SCIENCE BEHIND IT!

Stalactites and stalagmites are columns of stone that form underground in caves. They are made from minerals dissolved in rainwater that drips slowly from the walls and roofs of caves. The water evaporates as it drips. The dissolved minerals left behind form these unique structures. In this experiment, the baking soda acts the same way as dissolved minerals.

GLACIER POWER!

Glaciers are large, thick, slow-moving rivers of ice that carved valleys and have even created mountains. They weren't just part of the Ice Age—they still exist today! Over many years, fallen snow weighs down on layers below it. If the snow stays in place long enough, ice forms to make a glacier. A glacier can be as short as a football field or over 60 miles (100 km) long.

An "old" glacier looks blue!

As the weight of the ice increases, a glacier may move. Glaciers can move down hills or across any place with little **friction**. When glaciers move, they carry material such as dirt and rocks with them. They can also carve the land beneath them. Glaciers are so heavy that the changes they bring can be huge. Valleys created by glaciers often have steep cliffs. **Cirques** are landforms created when glaciers move backwards. They create hollows like shallow bowls. Horns are created when several glaciers erode a mountain until just a steep, pointed peak is left.

Glaciers by the Numbers

- 10% of Earth's land is covered with glaciers.
- Glaciers store about 75% of the fresh water in the world.
- If all the ice in glaciers melted, the seas around the world would rise about 30 feet (70 m).
- You can find glaciers on every continent except Australia. Even Africa has glaciers! Antarctica and Greenland have most of the world's glacial ice.

WHAT COLOR IS THE ICE?

Icicles look clear, but glaciers can have different colors. A glacier that appears white usually has tiny air bubbles throughout the ice. An "old" glacier can look blue. When the ice is pressed for years and years, the air pockets between ice crystals get smaller until they disappear completely. The ice absorbs all the other colors in the **spectrum** and reflects blue. The less air in the ice, the more blue is reflected.

Make a Glacier Model

Glaciers are mighty forces, traveling over land. Learn more about how a glacier moves—and what it leaves in its path.

You will need:

- [ ] 12 inch (30 cm) square of aluminum foil
- [ ] water
- [ ] an ice cube
- [ ] sand (about a spoonful)
- [ ] a lump of modeling clay
- [ ] paper towel
- [ ] pencil and paper

1. Use a 12-inch (30 cm) square piece of aluminum foil to make a box shape with edges about 2 inches (5 cm) high. Fill it with water and freeze it overnight.

2. Remove the block from the freezer and unwrap the foil. Rub the ice block over some modeling clay. What happens?

3. Press the ice cube gently into the surface of the clay. Move the ice cube back and forth 3-4 times. What happens?

4. Make a small pile of sand on top of the clay. Put the ice cube on the sand over the clay. Let it sit for about a minute.

5. Remove the ice cube and take a look at the surface that was on the sand. Put it back into position. Move it back and forth on the sandy surface of the clay 3-4 times.

6. Take off the ice cube. Using a paper towel, wipe the extra sand off the surface of the clay. Examine the clay. How does it look now as compared to when you began the experiment?

Glaciers . . . and Us!

- **In La Paz, Bolivia, melting ice from a nearby ice cap provides drinking water during dry spells.**
- **In many places around the world, people have used melted glacial water to create electricity.**
- **In many parts of the world, glaciers are shrinking because of global warming.**

THE SCIENCE BEHIND IT!

Glaciers are giant sheets of ice that are constantly moving in slow motion over land. In hundreds of thousands of years, this process can wear away a mountain until it is level with a flat plain. The movement of glaciers has helped to carve out the world's continents.

VOLCANOES
Landforms that Explode

When you hear *volcano,* you might think of a mountain with hot ash and fire spewing from the top. But not all volcanoes are mountains. A volcano is any place on the surface of the planet where melted rock, gases, and fiery debris erupt or ooze through Earth's crust. Some are cracks in the Earth, some are domes, some are shields, some are mountains . . . but they all start in the same place.

BEGINNING WITH . . . . EARTH!

Earth's surface is called the crust. It is made of **solid** rock. Below the crust is Earth's mantle. The mantle is very hot. Sometimes the heat melts the rock in the Earth's crust.

Crust
Mantle
Solid inner core
Liquid outer core

Some volcanoes erupt in a big blast, spitting out hot lava.

VOLCANIC ERUPTIONS

Volcanoes form when melted rock reaches the Earth's surface. We call the melted rock lava. Volcanoes erupt, pouring out hot lava, gases, and ash. Sometimes a volcanic eruption is like a big blast. Others volcanoes simply ooze lava for a very long time. Either way, eruptions can cause damage to property and loss of life.

Changing the Face of Earth?

Volcanoes change Earth's surface in many different ways. Volcanoes create new land by bringing melted rock from deep inside Earth to the surface. Volcanic eruptions can blow the top off a mountain. Volcanoes can spit out tons of ash, covering large areas of land—even entire cities!

Dome
Magma

Volcanoes may begin under the ocean's surface.

Make a Volcano Model

You can make a volcano "erupt" in the safety of your own home.

You will need:

- baking soda
- vinegar
- red colored gelatin powder
- 8 oz. drinking glass
- plate
- teaspoon

1 Put a plate underneath a drinking glass for the overflow from your volcano.

2 Pour vinegar into the glass, about 2/3 full.

3 Add 4 tsp. of gelatin powder to the glass.

4 Get ready to watch. Add 2 tsp. of baking soda to the mixture in the glass.

5 Watch your volcano erupt!

Volcano Extremes!

- Earth's largest volcano, at 6 miles tall, is Hawaii's Mauna Loa.
- In the solar system, the "largest volcano" prize goes to Olympus Mons, a volcano on Mars that is 17 miles tall and over 300 miles from edge to edge.
- Several volcanoes compete for "most active," but one of them, Stromboli Volcano, has been erupting almost continually for over 2,000 years off the coast of southern Italy.

THE SCIENCE BEHIND IT!

Volcanic eruptions occur when there is a hole or break in the Earth's crust that allows liquid rock from deep underground to escape to the surface. Just like your volcano model, liquid flows down the side of the volcano. In a real volcano, however, this liquid is red-hot lava. (The eruption in this experiment is caused by an acid-base reaction. See page 66!) Scientists called "volcanologists" study the changes that take place in lava flows to understand and try to predict when volcano eruptions will happen.

Feel the Earth Move

PLATE TECTONICS

You probably wouldn't recognize Earth if you saw it 200 million years ago. Scientists think that, back then, all the major continents formed one giant supercontinent. The continent in this **theory** is called **Pangaea**. When you look at a world map today, you see continents, oceans, and a few islands. It looks as if the super continent, Pangaea, broke apart. The pieces would fit back together if you could move them.

Did continents look like this long ago?

PLATE TECTONICS

Earth's surface is made up of **plates**, or pieces of the Earth's outer crust. **Plate tectonics** is the study of how these plates move. The plates usually move very slowly, bumping, pushing, or sliding along lines called faults. You usually don't feel these movements. After all, it took over millions of years for Earth's surface to look like it does today. What can happen if the plates move suddenly? Earthquakes!

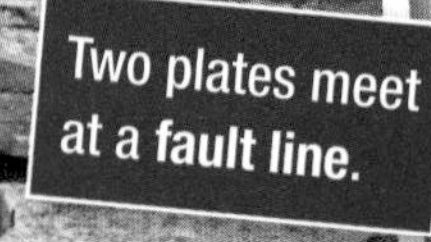
Two plates meet at a **fault line**.

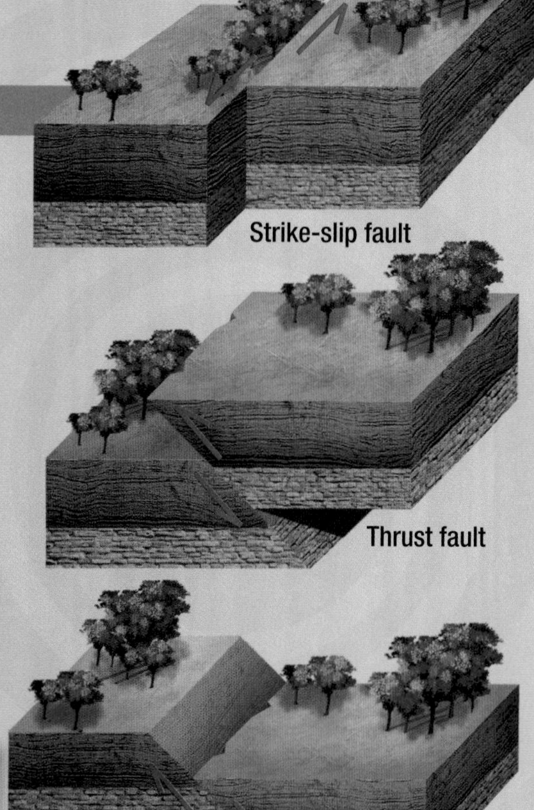

Plates move in different ways.

Making Waves

Earthquakes can have another effect—a huge wave called a tsunami! Model a tsunami in a pan.

You will need:

- a large, deep pan
- water
- 2 wooden blocks

1 Place two blocks into the large, deep pan.

2 Fill the pan with enough water to cover the blocks.

3 Sink the blocks and clap them together under the water.

4 Observe. What did the water do when the two blocks smashed together?

The Ring of Fire

Volcanoes and earthquakes occur where Earth's tectonic plates meet. The Ring of Fire is one of the best-known areas for volcanic activity. It is a horseshoe-shaped area in the Pacific Ocean. The Ring of Fire has over 400 volcanoes and is home to over three-fourths of the world's **dormant** volcanoes. The area also experiences ninety percent of the world's earthquakes. Now that's shaky—and explosive—ground!

THE SCIENCE BEHIND IT!

You created a model of a **tsunami**! A tsunami is a large wall of water that develops when there is an earthquake under the ocean. An earthquake involves the moving of the tectonic plates. This movement causes great amounts of water to be **compressed** so tightly that a giant wave forms. The experiment simulates what happens in real life. When the two blocks were "clapped" together, the water pushed up and up until it made a giant wave. Tsunamis can reach 50 to 100 feet (15-30 m) high and can threaten villages, towns, and cities that are close to the ocean.

What Makes CLIMATE?

Why is the desert hot and dry? Why are some places in the world forests and others grasslands? Why do some plants and animals live in some parts of the world and others thrive in other places? The answer is **climate**. Climate is the long-term weather of an area, usually over a period of 30 years or longer. Two important parts of a climate are the amount of **precipitation** (rain or snow) and the usual temperature.

THE "RECIPE" FOR CLIMATE

What makes climate?

- Latitude: The further from the **equator**, the larger the temperature difference is between winter and summer.
- Terrain: The higher a place is, the colder it is.
- Water: Near large bodies of water, the winters are milder and the summers are cooler.
- Wind: Global winds shift during the different seasons. In spring, winds move toward the poles. In the fall, they move toward the equator.

Here are a few types of climates:

TROPICAL WET CLIMATES

Tropical wet climates are hot and humid all year round. The average rainfall can top 100 inches (254 cm) in a year.

ICE CAP CLIMATES

Climates on the **polar** ice caps are the coldest climates on Earth. Temperatures don't go above freezing, even in summer.

DESERT CLIMATES

Desert climates have huge temperature differences between night and day. They have very little precipitation.

Tropical wet climates are perfect for trees!

Penguins live in cold climates.

Not all deserts are hot, but all are dry.

Bring on the Heat!

When you build this "heat wave in a jar," you'll find out more about the greenhouse effect.

You will need:

- 2 large glass jars, same size
- 1 jar lid
- 2 pieces of black paper or black cloth
- 2 thermometers that will fit inside the jars
- oven mitts
- a very sunny day

1. Place a piece of paper or cloth in each jar.

2. Next, put a thermometer in each jar. Place the jars outside in a sunny location.

3. Put the lid on one of the jars.

4. Record the temperatures in both jars. Record the temperature every two minutes for 20 minutes.

5. Use the oven mitts to move the jars to the shade. Remove the lid from the covered jar.

6. Compare the temperatures of the two jars. Is there a big difference between them?

The Greenhouse Effect

There is a layer of gases building up around the Earth called greenhouse gases. Some of the heat in sunlight is reflected toward the atmosphere as infrared radiation. Greenhouse gases soak up the infrared radiation and trap it in Earth's atmosphere. Some scientists say the greenhouse effect is warming up the Earth. This can lead to climate changes and the melting of the polar ice.

Greenhouse

THE SCIENCE BEHIND IT!

You made a model of the greenhouse effect! Sunlight heats up the objects on which it shines. An object on the inside of a closed container heats quickly, because the heat cannot escape. The closed jar holds in heat from the Sun's rays. The temperature in this jar rose much more quickly than the jar without a lid. Greenhouses use this science to keep the air warm for their plants.

The Four SEASONS

In some places, winter brings snow.

You live in North America, and you're shivering in the winter cold. Why is it cold? Does it get cold in the winter because the Sun and Earth move apart from each other? Actually, the Earth's seasons are NOT caused by differences in the distance from the Sun throughout the year. The seasons happen because the Earth is tilted.

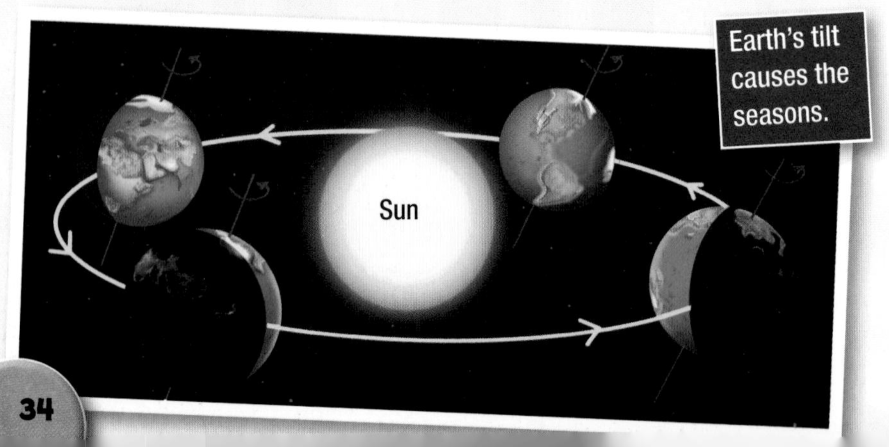

Earth's tilt causes the seasons.

TILT!

When you picture the Earth, with its north and south poles, you might picture it "straight up and down." But the imaginary line that connects the poles, the **axis** of the Earth, does not go straight up and down. It tilts. The tilting gives us the seasons. In the summer, for example, the Sun's rays hit part of Earth at a more direct angle. The days are much longer than the nights. In winter, the tilt of the Earth makes the Sun's rays hit that same part of Earth at a different angle. The days are short and cold.

What Causes Seasons?

With this activity, you can see the reason for seasons.

You will need:

- flashlight
- white paper

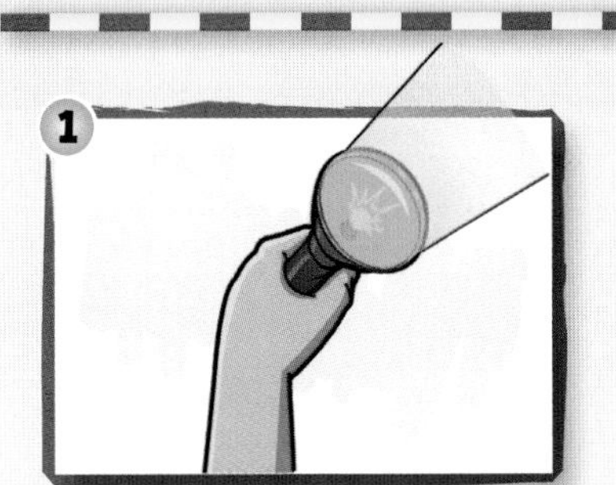

1. Turn on the flashlight and hold it in one hand.

2. Hold the sheet of paper upright in your other hand facing the light beam. What shape does the light beam make on the paper?

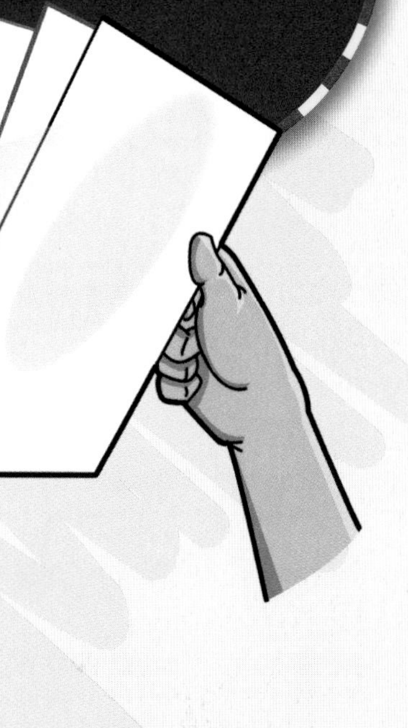

3. Tilt the top of the paper away from the flashlight. Try to keep the paper the same distance from the flashlight as before. What shape does the light beam make on the paper?

Do the same, this time tilting the bottom of the paper away from the flashlight.

The Seasons . . . and You!

If you live in an area in which the seasons change, you know that they have a direct impact on your life. The seasons affect the clothes you wear, the activities you do, and even the foods available for you to eat! Some seasons require a little more safety. In the summer, the rays of the Sun damage your skin, so you need to protect yourself. Winter can bring ice—don't slip and fall!

THE SCIENCE BEHIND IT!

You just modeled the Sun shining on Earth! When you tilt the paper away from the flashlight, the circle of light will change shape from a circle to an oval. The light will spread out from the center and will become less bright around the edges. The Earth is tilted and spins on its axis around the Sun. This tilt affects how much sunlight an area receives. When the top is tilted toward to the Sun, the top half of the Earth has summer. As the Earth travels around the Sun, the same part of the Earth tilts away from the Sun little by little, causing the top half of the Earth to have winter.

All About the WEATHER

Weather can ruin a picnic or make a day at the beach even better. It can create beautiful "pictures" in the sky from white fluffy clouds. Weather forecasters use terms like ***fronts*** and *pressure*. What are they talking about? Let's find out more.

What makes great weather like this?

This weather map shows high and low pressure areas.

Amazing Science!

Cities create their own weather. Scientists are studying the consequences of the fact that, as cities grow, buildings and paved surfaces replace the natural landscape and can soak up heat to raise air temperatures by as much as 10° F (12° C). This bubble of heat is called an "urban heat island."

IT'S ALL ABOUT AIR

You might hear weather forecasts about a cold front coming in. With the cold **front**, temperatures will plunge. But what is a cold front exactly? Fronts are borders between air masses. An air mass is just a large body of air that has similar temperature and amount of moisture in the entire mass.

When air masses meet, they create a front. In a cold front, for example, a cold air mass is moving in to replace a warm air mass. The winds usually shift, too. Before a cold front comes through, the winds blow from the south. After the cold front, the winds may blow from the north instead.

CLOUDS

Clouds are an important part of the weather. A cloud is a collection of tiny droplets of water or ice crystals in the air.

Scientists classify clouds according to how high they are above Earth, their shape, and what they're made of.

Cirrus clouds are highest above the ground. They are so high, they are made of ice. These clouds are thin and wispy.

Alto clouds are the middle clouds. They are made of ice crystals and water droplets. They usually cover the entire sky and can signal approaching thunderstorms.

Stratus clouds are the lowest clouds. They look like fog that's just higher than the ground. Sometimes light mist falls from these clouds.

Cumulus clouds aren't classified by their height. The clouds are flat on the bottom and rounded on the top. If you see those round parts grow taller, watch out! The clouds signal that heavy rain, snow, hail, or even tornadoes are on the way.

Thunderstorms can leave damage in their wake.

THUNDER AND LIGHTNING!

There's definitely a recipe for a thunderstorm. It takes unstable air and moisture. You also need something that lifts unstable air, like a front, a strong breeze, or even a mountain. Thunderstorms can happen anytime, although they usually happen in warm weather and in the afternoon and evening. All thunderstorms have **lightning**, and lightning is dangerous! Lightning kills more people every year than hurricanes or tornadoes.

Stay Safe in Thunderstorms

If you're *outdoors*:

- **The best place to be is inside. If you are in the car, close the windows.**
- **If you can't find shelter, stay away from trees. You are safer in an open area.**
- **Avoid metal. Drop your backpack.**
- **Don't go in the water.**

If you're already *indoors*:

- **Avoid water, because it conducts electricity.**
- **Do not use electric appliances. They conduct electricity, too.**
- **Stay away from windows and doors.**

Collecting the Rain

Billions of drops of water combine to form one cloud. Using a rain gauge, meteorologists measure how much rain falls. Check out how to build your own rain gauge and start measuring rain fall in your backyard!

You will need:

- 2-L plastic bottle
- 2 cups (0.5 L) of sand
- scissors
- permanent marker
- ruler

1. Ask an adult to cut off the top of the soda bottle just before it begins to taper.

2. Pour 2 cups (0.5 L) of sand into the bottle. Pour enough water into the bottle to cover the sand. This will keep your rain gauge from falling over.

3. Using a marker, draw a level with the wet sand. Mark the line with a "0." This is where the measurements will start.

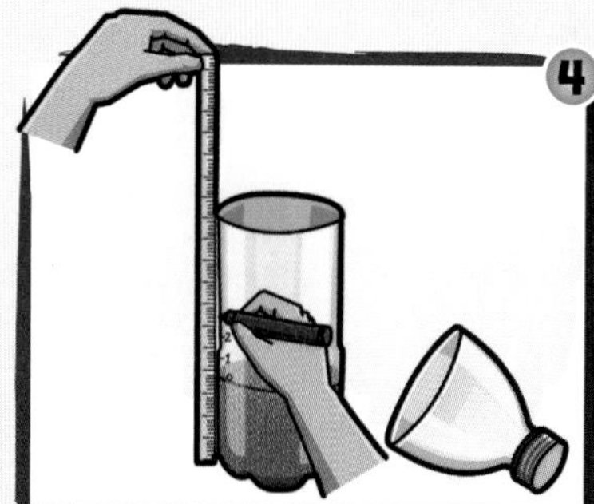

4. Use a ruler to measure 1" (2.5 cm), 2" (5 cm), and 3" (7.6 cm) up the bottle from the baseline. Draw a line at each inch mark and label the lines. To make your rain gauge more accurate, mark smaller measures, such as half-inches or centimeters.

5. Flip the cut-off portion of the bottle upside down and insert it into the bottle. This will cause the water to be funneled from the top of the bottle into the bottom of the bottle and prevent the water from evaporating.

Place the rain gauge in an open area outside and record the amount of water in the bottle after each rainfall.

The "official" rain gauge used by the United States Weather Bureau is a 19.7 inch (50 cm) tall cylinder with a 7.9 inch (20 cm) diameter funnel. Official rain gauges have a housing to protect the measuring cylinder inside so that the measurement is very accurate.

Measure the Pressure

You hear the forecaster say, "Barometric pressure will rise," but what exactly does that mean?

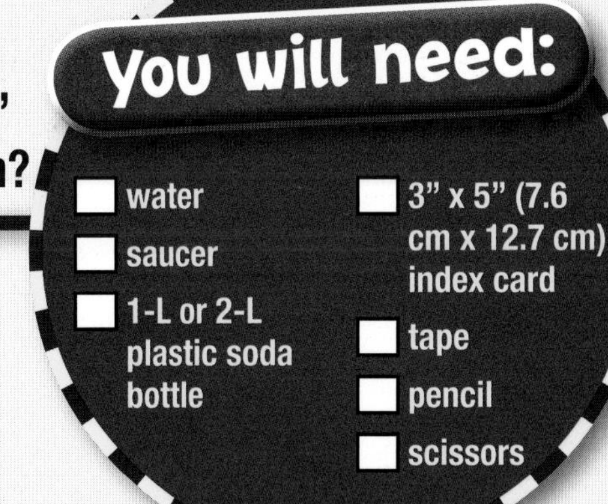

you will need:

- water
- saucer
- 1-L or 2-L plastic soda bottle
- 3" x 5" (7.6 cm x 12.7 cm) index card
- tape
- pencil
- scissors

1

Pour water into the bottle until it is about three-quarters full.

2

Fill the saucer halfway with water. With your thumb over the mouth of the bottle, turn the bottle upside down and hold it in the water in the saucer.

3

Make sure the mouth of the bottle is under the surface of the water in the saucer. Remove your thumb and rest the bottle upside down in the saucer.

4

Cut the index card into thin strips. Place a strip of index card vertically along the outside of the bottle, toward the top. Tape it in place.

5 Using your pencil, gently mark the level of water on your index card, and write the date next to your mark.

For the next few days, repeat step 5. What do you notice?

THE SCIENCE BEHIND IT!

The weight of the air in our atmosphere presses down on the water in the saucer, keeping water inside the bottle. The weight of the air in the atmosphere and the force it exerts is called air pressure. Air pressure changes slightly from day to day. When there is a decrease in air pressure, the water level drops. An increase sends the water up. When the level of the water inside the bottle drops, you can expect warmer, wetter weather!

TWISTERS!

What Makes a Tornado?

They fascinate and scare us at the same time. They are violent, yet some people think they are beautiful. They have the power to destroy and even kill. What are they? **Tornadoes**!

A tornado leaves a path of destruction.

Tornadoes spiral down from thunderclouds. They pick up dust and debris.

When Is a Tornado not a Tornado?

A tornado is not a tornado until it hits the ground. If the tornado stays up in the clouds, it's technically a funnel. A tornado over water is called a waterspout. A strong waterspout can flip over a boat, but waterspouts are usually weaker than land tornadoes.

HOW DO TORNADOES WORK?

Watch water draining from your bathtub—you'll see a spiral formation called a **vortex**. Gravity creates suction, pulling water particles in. Water particles accelerate toward the point of the suction. They also flow with the other particles around them. The spiral creates a strong vortex. In a tornado, the same kind of thing happens. The particles are made of air instead of water.

Tornado in a Bottle

The spinning column of air in a tornado is called a vortex. You can make a vortex in a soda bottle!

You will need:

- ☐ two 2-liter soda bottles with caps
- ☐ duct tape
- ☐ water
- ☐ drill (get an adult's help with this)
- ☐ food coloring (optional)

1

Take the caps off both the soda bottles. Have an adult help you drill a 1/2" hole in the center of each bottle cap.

2

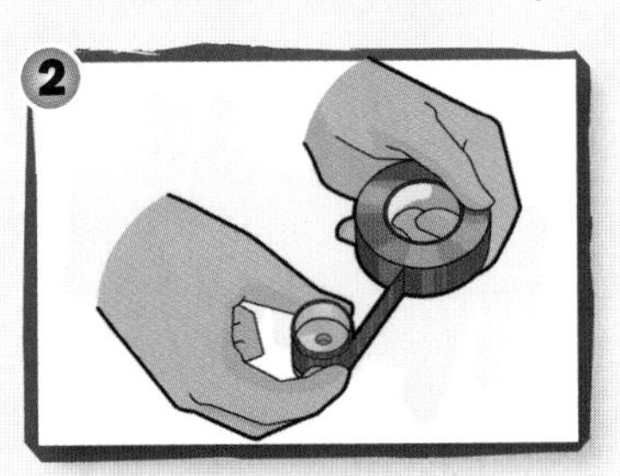

Wrap a piece of duct tape around the outside of the two caps to join them together.

3

Screw the double cap onto one of the soda bottles.

4

Fill the other bottle about 3/4 full of water. Add a few drops of food coloring to help you get a better view of the vortex.

5

Screw the empty bottle onto the top of the bottle containing the water. Hold the duct-taped area with one hand and the bottom of the bottle with the other hand.

6

Vortex

Turn the bottles upside-down. Swirl them in a few quick circles. You'll see the vortex when the water drains from one bottle to another.

Where in the World Are Tornadoes?

Tornadoes occur in many parts of the world but they strike most often in the United States. An area between the Rockies and the Appalachian Mountains is nicknamed "Tornado Alley" because it has so many tornadoes in the spring and summer.

THE SCIENCE BEHIND IT!

The water needs to flow from a large space into a much smaller one. The force of the water creates suction. The swirl of the water in the bottle is the same as the swirl of the air in a tornado.

The Eye Of The Storm: HURRICANES

A **hurricane** is one big storm! It starts over the sea. It can be over 600 miles (about 1000 km) wide with winds that travel up to 200 miles per hour (about 320 kph). A hurricane usually lasts for more than a week before it travels over enough land to slow it down. It causes heavy rains, strong winds, and lots of damage to the land. Where do hurricanes come from?

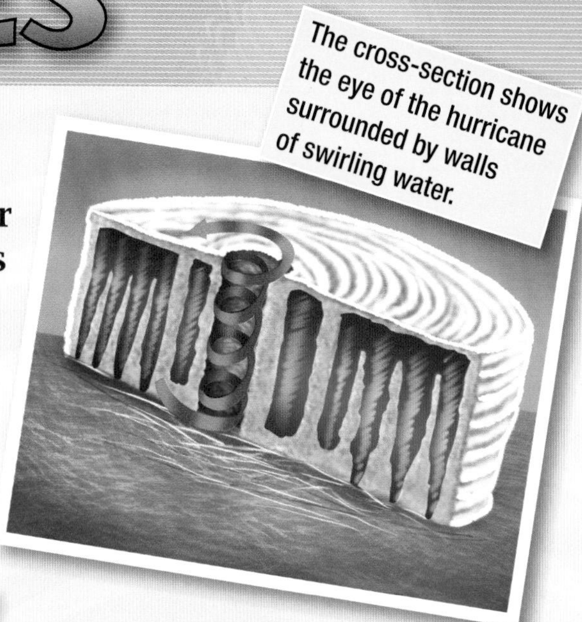

The cross-section shows the eye of the hurricane surrounded by walls of swirling water.

This top view of a hurricane shows the eye of the storm.

HOW THEY FORM

Hurricanes form only over warm ocean water. The water has to be at least 80° F (26.7° C). Warm, moist air is like fuel for hurricanes. The warm, moist air over the ocean's surface rises. The air pressure below this is low. Then surrounding air pushes in to the low-pressure area. The new air becomes warm and rises, too. This system of clouds continues to grow and spin, fueled by the heat of the ocean and the moist air continuing to rise. The storm system rotates. An "eye" forms in the middle.

Rating Hurricanes

The category of a hurricane is the hurricane's strength. Why is it important for people to classify hurricanes? Knowing the strength of the hurricane might let people in its path know what to expect—and to prepare for what's coming.

Category	Wind Speed (mph/kph)	Amount of Expected Damage
1	74-95 (119-153 kph)	minimal
2	96-110 (154-177 kph)	moderate
3	111-130 (178-209 kph)	extensive
4	131-155 (210-249 kph)	extreme
5	156 (250 kph) and higher	catastrophic

THE SURGE

As a hurricane swirls around and around, the air isn't the only thing affected. The water is affected too. The spiral winds push the water together into a big mound. When a hurricane hits land, this water piles up and is pushed right onto the land. This is called a **storm surge**. If the ocean floor slopes gradually to the shore, the storm surge is really damaging. The rise in sea level can destroy the land along the shore.

Water rises in a surge that hits land.

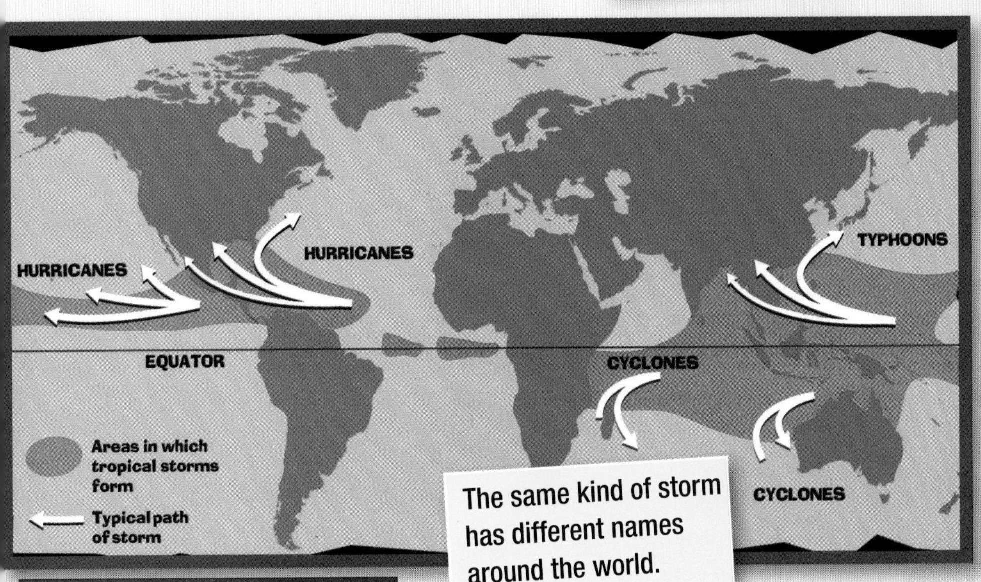

The same kind of storm has different names around the world.

WHERE IN THE WORLD?

If a storm forms in the Atlantic Ocean, the Gulf of Mexico, or the eastern Pacific Ocean . . . it's called a **hurricane**.

...If that same kind of storm forms in the western Pacific Ocean . . . it's called a **typhoon**.

...If that same kind of storm forms in the Indian Ocean, the Bay of Bengal, or near Australia . . . it's called a **cyclone**.

EXTREME HURRICANES

- In 1972, Hurricane Agnes hit Florida. It had extremely high floodwaters. The floods stretched from Florida all the way to New York.
- In 1938, a hurricane hit the New England area. This area hardly ever has hurricanes, so people didn't believe that a hurricane was on its way. But the storm hit, surprising people who lived there. In today's dollars, the damage topped $3 billion.
- In 1900, people who lived on Galveston, a small island off the Texas coast, saw the storm flags warning of a hurricane. The hurricane came to shore quickly, and the huge storm surge flooded the island. Thousands of people died.

What Good Is a Hurricane?

- Tropical storms sometimes end droughts, or long periods without rain. In 1996, Hurricane Dolly damaged parts of Mexico. But it also brought rain that was badly needed to Texas, ending a severe drought.
- Hurricanes help maintain the heat balance of the Earth. By moving warm air from the ocean, hurricanes cool the tropics and bring warmer air to cooler places.

Swirling Vortex

You can see it when you flush a toilet. You can see it when you blow into a straw that's submerged in liquid. What is it? It's a vortex! And it's part of the science behind hurricanes.

You will need:

- 18-oz. (237 ml) drinking glass
- water
- straw

1 Fill the glass with water.

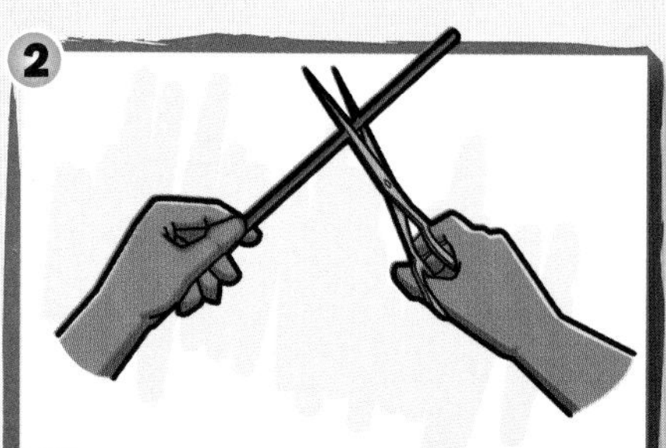

2 Make a horizontal snip in the mid-point of the straw. Do not cut all the way through the straw!

3 Put the straw in the glass.

4 Blow into the straw.

What do you notice about the water?

What's in a Name?

Today all hurricanes have names. Names help us identify and track storms. In 1953, the National Weather Service started giving women's names to storms. Men's names were added in 1979. Every year, the World Meteorological Society decides the storms' names. They have a name for every letter in the alphabet except Q, U, and Z. If a hurricane is very deadly, the name is "retired."

THE SCIENCE BEHIND IT!

When you blow through the straw, some air escapes through the slit. This reduces the air pressure at the bottom of the straw. The swirling you saw in the glass is like a hurricane When a hurricane develops, a swirling vortex moves from the surface of the water to the upper atmosphere. When this vortex becomes powerful enough, it becomes a hurricane.

Hurricane in a Jar

Make a hurricane safely at home so you can see these magnificent storms at work.

You will need:

- a glass jar with lid
- water
- food coloring
- liquid dish detergent
- vinegar

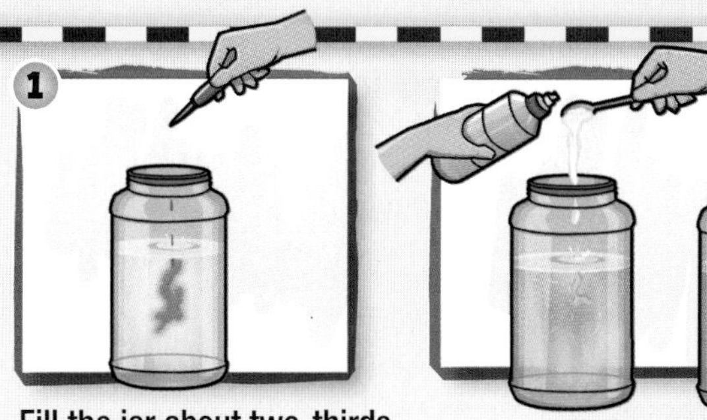

1. Fill the jar about two-thirds full with water. Put a few drops of food coloring in the water.
2. Add 1 teaspoon of dish detergent and 1 teaspoon of vinegar.

3. Screw the lid on tightly.
4. Shake the jar and then twist it to make the liquid inside spin.

THE SCIENCE BEHIND IT!

The spinning vortex looks like a miniature hurricane. Hurricanes form over tropical waters because the air is moist and warm. Hurricane wind speeds range from 74 miles per hour (119 km/h) to 180 miles per hour (290 km/h). In this activity, both the jar and the liquid are moving. The inner liquids keep spinning and the outer liquids slow down when you stop moving the jar. This creates a vortex that can be seen for just a few seconds. For more fun, try adding some glitter to the liquid and see what happens!

Meet the Hurricane Hunters!

If you knew a hurricane was coming, you'd try to move out of its path. But Hurricane Hunters actually fly their planes right into the eyes of these amazing storms. The 53rd Weather Reconnaissance Squadron is part of the Air Force Reserve. The Hurricane Hunters measure wind speed and barometric pressure, and get other information about the storm. These dangerous missions help the National Weather Service better predict the direction in which hurricanes are traveling, saving countless lives and properties.

This plane flies into hurricanes to measure wind speed.

OUR OCEANS

About 70% of our planet is covered with oceans, and 98% of the water on Earth is salt water. The average depth of the oceans is several thousand feet. Yet for all of the ocean surrounding us, the seafloor has been almost as mysterious as the surface of Mars because it is hard to explore!

The ocean floor has hills, mountains, and valleys.

Oceans carry energy in waves!

THE OCEAN FLOOR

On land, we have mountains, valleys, and plains. There are similar landforms under water. The **continental shelf** is a shelf that creates shallow water all around the edges of the oceans. At the edge of the shelf are steep slopes that drop to the deep ocean floor, the **abyssal plain**. The plain has huge underwater mountains. The world's longest mountain chains, in fact, are in the Atlantic and Indian Oceans.

WHAT ARE TIDES?

Twice a day, the ocean water at a shoreline is at its highest. Twice a day, the same water falls to its lowest level. **Tides** are the rising and falling of the sea. They are caused by the pull of the Moon's gravity on the oceans' waters as Earth spins around. The Moon's gravity has a pull on Earth. Earth's gravity holds everything on Earth. But the gravitational pull of the Moon is too strong for the Earth to hold all that water still. The ocean rises and falls because of the Moon's gravity.

Water moves on and off shore because of tides.

Ocean Motion!

What does the motion of a wave look like? Observe with a wave in a bottle.

You will need:

- a plastic bottle with a lid (like a 1-L or 2-L soda bottle)
- vegetable oil
- water
- blue food coloring

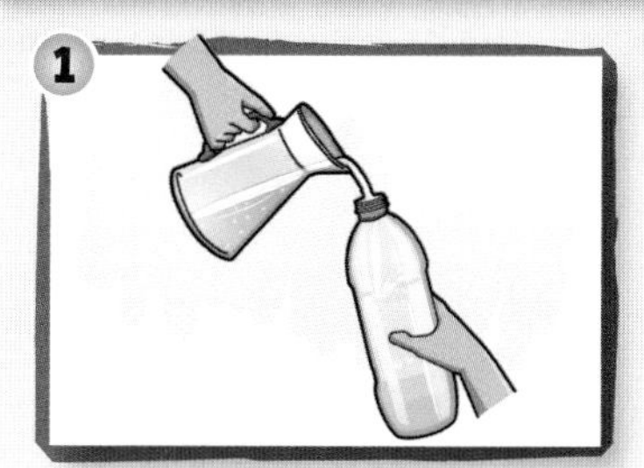

1. Fill your bottle about 2/3 with water.

2. Add a few drops of blue food coloring to the water.

3. Fill the bottle the rest of the way with vegetable oil.

4. Screw on the lid or cap the bottle very tightly.

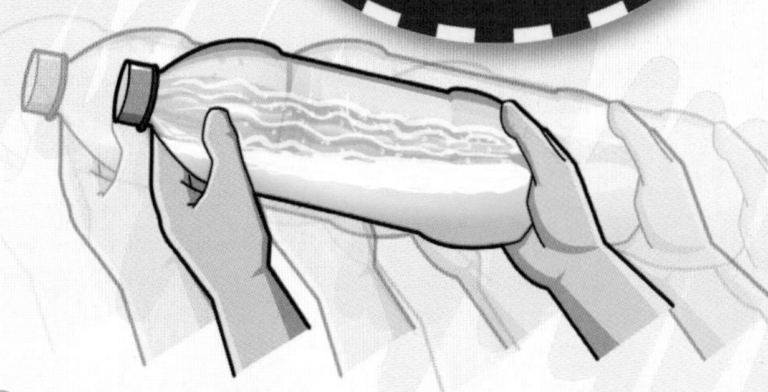

5. Hold your bottle on its side and tilt it back and forth slowly. What happens? How many waves can you make?

MEET *ALVIN*

Alvin is the name of a small deep-sea submarine. *Alvin* can reach depths of more than 14,000 feet (4,267 m). In 1966, it was used to find a hydrogen bomb after a plane crash. Scientist Robert D. Ballard used *Alvin* to find giant tubeworms and other amazing creatures 7,000 feet (2,134 m) under water. *Alvin* even found the sunken remains of the *Titanic*, a ship that sank more than 12,000 feet (3,658 m) under the cold waters of the northern Atlantic Ocean.

Alvin travels deep beneath the ocean's surface.

THE SCIENCE BEHIND IT!

Waves in the ocean are movements that carry energy from one place to another. Waves need to travel through a medium like water. When you see a wave, the water doesn't cause the waves. The energy in the water causes the waves to form. In this experiment, the energy for the waves in the bottle came from you.

WHAT IS PHYSICAL SCIENCE?

Why do moving things slow down and eventually stop? When some chemicals combine, why do they explode? What is the difference between temperature and heat? What is light, and why do we see different colors? What are the different types of matter in the universe?

How are these bright lights part of physical science?

Gears use simple machines to do work.

Wind can create energy.

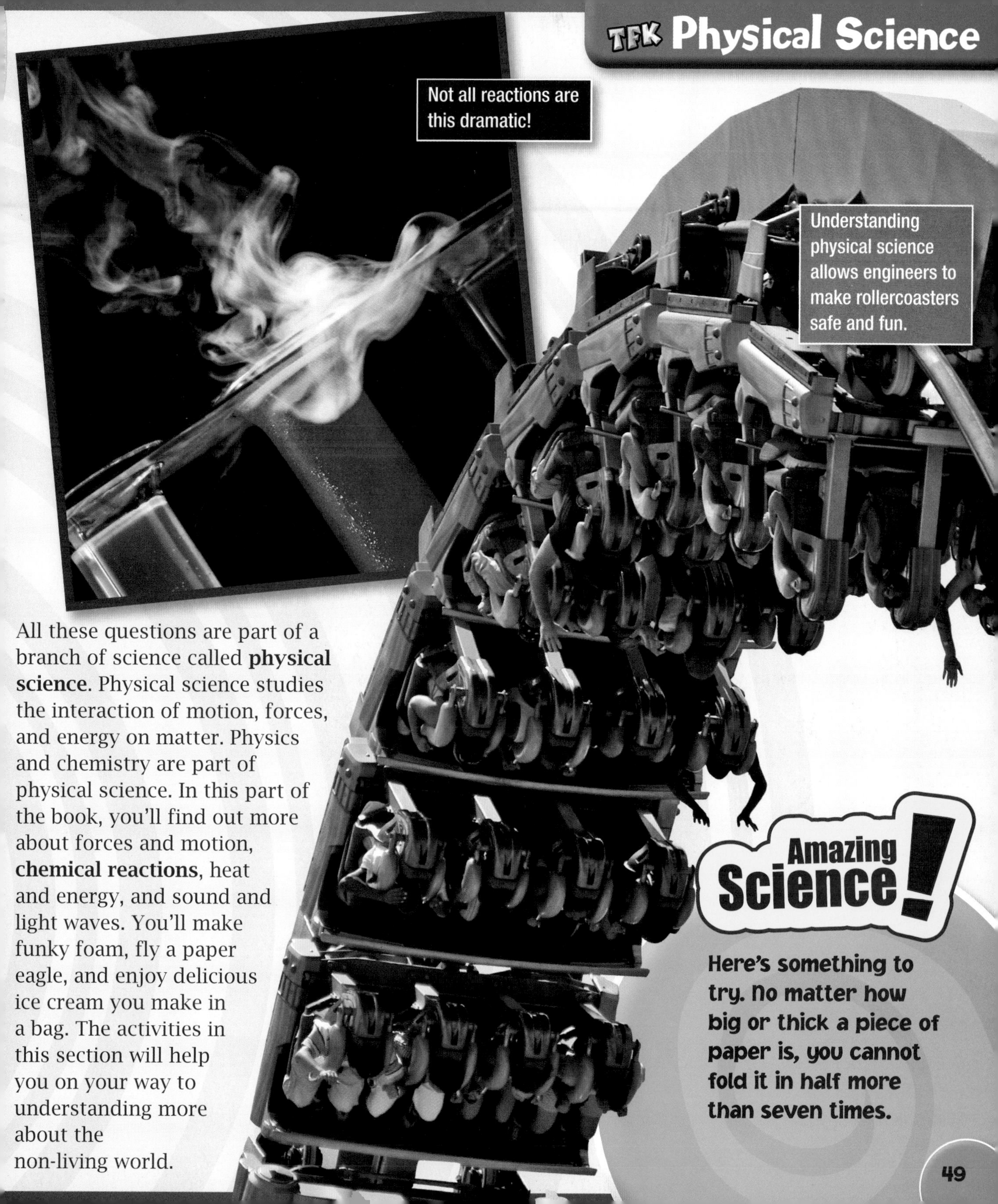

All these questions are part of a branch of science called **physical science**. Physical science studies the interaction of motion, forces, and energy on matter. Physics and chemistry are part of physical science. In this part of the book, you'll find out more about forces and motion, **chemical reactions**, heat and energy, and sound and light waves. You'll make funky foam, fly a paper eagle, and enjoy delicious ice cream you make in a bag. The activities in this section will help you on your way to understanding more about the non-living world.

Amazing Science!

Here's something to try. No matter how big or thick a piece of paper is, you cannot fold it in half more than seven times.

Turn up the HEAT

You rub your hands together and feel your hands getting warmer. You are creating heat. But what exactly is heat? Where does it come from? Heat is another name for thermal energy. It's the energy stored inside a substance. When two substances with different amounts of internal energy are near each other, heat transfers from one substance to another.

HEAT MOVES

Heat moves in three ways: **conduction**, **convection**, and radiation.

- Conduction is the direct transfer of heat from one object to another. If you have walked across sand on a hot day, you've experienced conduction. Some materials, like metals, are good at conducting heat. Wood is not a good **conductor**.

Convection warms food on the stove.

Heat from the Sun travels to Earth by radiation.

- Convection is the transfer of heat from one area to another when matter moves. When you heat a pot of water on the stove, the hot water rises to the top of the pot and gives off energy. The air is heated by convection.
- **Radiation** is heat from invisible rays, like radio waves or ultraviolet light. The Sun's heat comes to Earth by radiation.

Temperature Scales

Temperature is a measure of how fast molecules move. Thermometers measure temperature. You measure your body temperature with a thermometer. Have you noticed that there's a thermometer on your oven? Scientists use thermometers in the lab, too.

Scale	Water Freezes	Water Boils	What else is important?
Fahrenheit	32°	212°	This scale divides the difference between the freezing and boiling points of water into 180 equal degrees.
Celsius	0°	100°	This is the Celius scale, with 100 degrees between the freezing point and boiling point of water.
Kelvin	273.15	373.13	This scale starts with absolute zero, the temperature at which no molecules move. Instead of saying "one degree Kelvin," you just say "one Kelvin."

What Makes a Good Conductor?

People who drive trains aren't the only conductors. Conductors are materials that allow heat to pass along or through them.

Cut out three pieces of paper all the same size, about 1-½ inches by ¾ inch (4 cm by 2 cm).

Tape each piece of paper to a toothpick to make three flags.

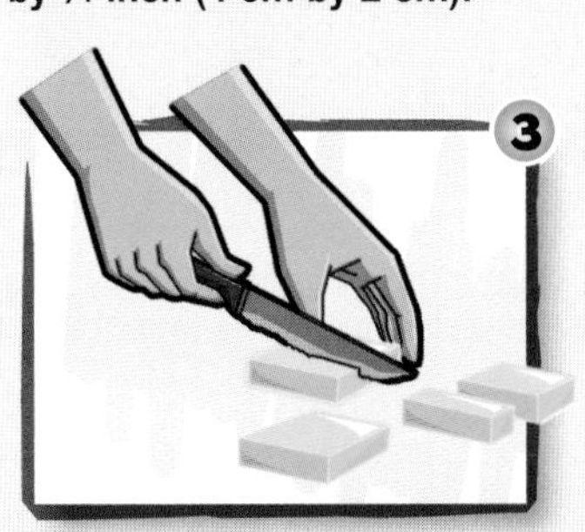

Cut three pieces of butter, margarine, or shortening with the plastic knife, making sure they are all about the same size.

Place one piece on the metal lid, one on the plastic lid, and one on the small piece of wood. Put a flag into each piece.

Ask an adult to help you put hot water into the large bowl or bucket. Place the lids and piece of wood gently in the water so they float.

6 Time how long it takes each piece of butter to melt and each flag to fall over.

Which piece melts the fastest? Which takes the longest to melt? How is this related to conduction of heat?

THE SCIENCE BEHIND IT!

The flag on the metal lid drops first, because the tiny molecules that make up the lid conduct heat very well. Heat energy moves quickly from water molecules to the molecules of a conductor and from there to the butter,, causing it to melt. The flag on the piece of wood is the last to fall. Why? Because molecules of wood are bad heat conductors.

GET ENERGIZED

Different Forms of Energy

Thermal energy is the kind of energy that is related to or caused by heat. What happens when thermal energy is applied to a substance? The speed of the molecules in the substance increases. As molecules move more quickly, the substance heats up. In a pot of boiling water, the heat of the stove makes the water molecules move more quickly. You can see the bubbles in the water as the molecules start to move.

Steam can power a huge locomotive.

SOLAR ENERGY

If your parents park their car in the sun, even on a cold day the Sun warms up the inside of the car through the windows. How does this happen? With **solar energy**! People have used solar energy for thousands of years. The ancient Greeks built houses that would allow the Sun's rays to enter in the winter. Romans realized that glass would allow light to pass through while trapping heat. It's only been in the past 50 years or so that we've used solar panels to capture the energy from the Sun and change it into electricity.

These panels collect and store the Sun's energy.

GETTING STEAMY

When you boil water, you make steam. How can that steam be harnessed into energy? That question has intrigued scientists and inventors for years. Thousands of years ago, a mathematician named Hero designed a simple steam engine. He proposed filling a hollow sphere with water and then putting the sphere over a fire. The heat would create steam that would be forced out through small holes. The sphere would rotate and make energy. That thousands-of-years-old technology was the basis for early steam engines used in trains and boats. Today, scientists are looking for new ways to use steam to create power without pollution.

Thermal Eagles

Make a bird out of paper, add some energy, and watch it fly.

- 1 white paper plate
- scissors
- glue
- thread
- paper
- colored pencils
- heat source such as a light bulb

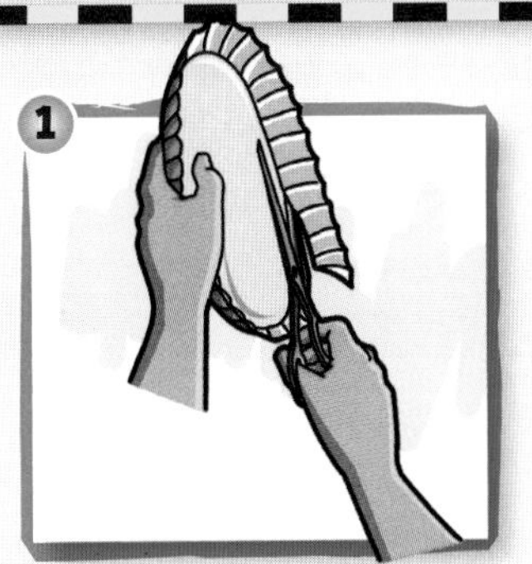

1 Cut the ribbed edge off the paper plate.

2 Start from the middle of the plate and draw a spiral about 1/2 inch (1 cm) wide. Cut along this line.

3 Draw four eagles on a sheet of paper. The eagles should each be about 5 inches wide and 3 inches tall. Color the pictures.

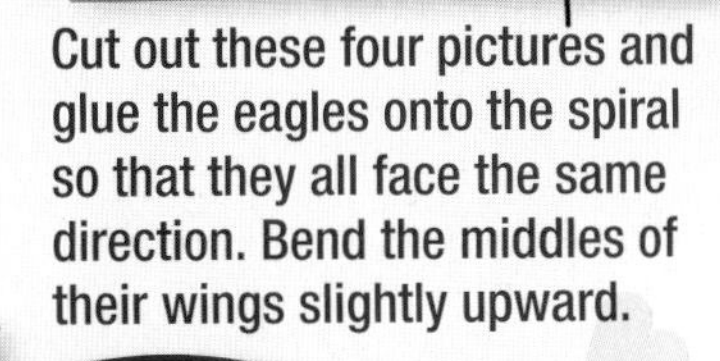

4 Cut out these four pictures and glue the eagles onto the spiral so that they all face the same direction. Bend the middles of their wings slightly upward.

5 Poke a small hole in the center of the spiral. Tie a thread through this hole and hang up your mobile over a heat source like a light bulb. (See safety note.)

Blowing Off Steam

Geysers are hot springs that erupt from the ground in streams of boiling water and steam. Geysers are hot because of geothermal energy, or heat that comes from below the ground. Rapidly moving water molecules change liquid water to steam, exerting tremendous pressures. The steam and boiling water can shoot as high as 400 feet (130 m) into the air.

You're using thermal energy. The paper spiral turns as the warm current of air from your heat source rises. The current of air is strong enough to push against the paper, making it move.

IT'S ELEMENT-ARY

The Periodic Table

Table salt contains sodium.

Gold is an element.

You have probably heard of both gold and oxygen, just two of the elements on the periodic table. Sodium is another element. Elements are pure substances. Elements can't be changed into anything simpler through chemical processes. The periodic table shows all the elements known on Earth.

THE PERIODIC TABLE

Each element on the periodic table is shown by an abbreviation. *O*, for example, represents oxygen. *Au* represents gold, and *K* represents potassium. The elements are listed by the number of **protons** in each **atom** of the element. The elements themselves are classified according to their characteristics, such as being a metal, or a gas, or a radioactive material.

METAL VS. NONMETAL

You use **metals** every day. We use metal in pots and pans, jewelry, furniture, and more. Over three-fourths of the elements on the periodic table are metals. Metals are shiny and are good conductors. Metals are also **malleable**: you can change their shapes in ways such as hitting them with a hammer. Only 18 elements in the periodic table are considered nonmetals. Nonmetals have properties different from metals. Many of them are very different from each other, too.

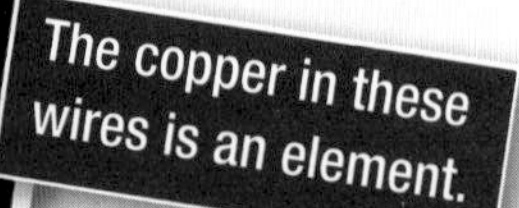

The copper in these wires is an element.

Organize the Elements

You can use other items to model a periodic table.

You will need:

- colored pencils
- colored markers
- colored crayons
- colored pens
- colored highlighters
- tape
- large sheet of paper
- ruler

1

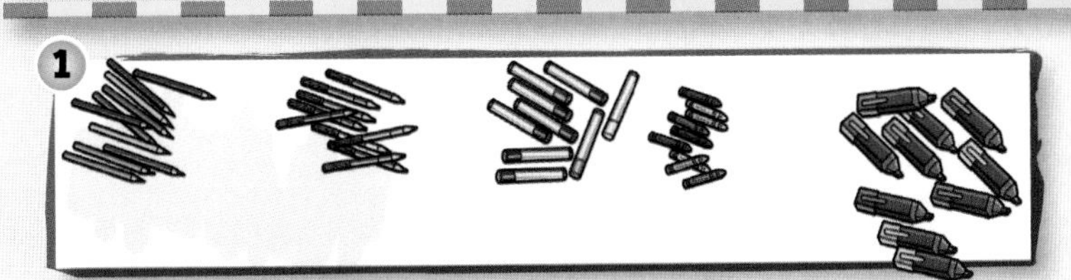

Separate the writing tools into groups: pencils, markers, highlighters, crayons, and pens.

2

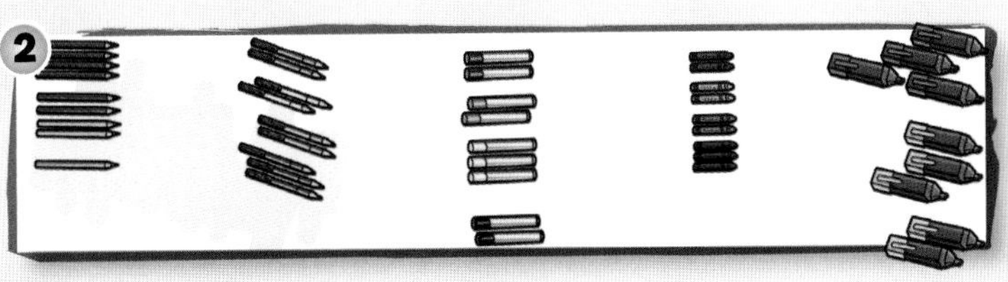

In each group, separate the writing tools according to the colors green, yellow, orange, red, blue, purple, black, and brown. Keep any writing tools that do not match these colors on the side.

3

Draw vertical lines on your paper to form six equal-sized columns.

4

Draw horizontal lines on your paper to form nine equal-sized rows.

5

Write the words *crayons, pencils, pens, markers,* and *highlighters* along the top row of columns 2 to 6. Write the colors *green, yellow, orange, red, blue, purple, black,* and *brown* in rows 2 to 9 in the left-most column.

6 Fill in each square with the right color. For example, you would use the green colored pencil to fill in the square in the column labeled pencils in the row labeled green.

Do you have writing tools that did not fit? Add more rows with the new colors.

Do you have empty squares? Try to find writing tools to fill the squares.

THE SCIENCE BEHIND IT!

Your table sorts writing tools by type and color. The periodic table of the elements sorts chemicals by mass and chemical properties. Scientists use the periodic table to find new elements. They search the periodic table for blank spots, and look for elements that fit the spot. Some scientists found elements that did not fit the table. They created new rows and columns to put the elements into the table.

CHEMICAL REACTIONS

The explosion of fireworks is caused by a chemical reaction.

You cut an apple in half. Have you changed the apple? It looks different, but it's made of the same things. You've created a physical change. A physical change happens when the form of something changes. What kind of change happens when fireworks explode in the sky? The exploding fireworks are a chemical change. One substance is changed into a different substance.

A SIMPLE REACTION

Chemical reactions can cause exploding fireworks, burn a match, and make your bread dough rise. Such reactions occur when two or more molecules interact and make something happen. You start with one substance and turn it into another. If you've seen a rusty bicycle, you've seen a chemical reaction. Iron in the bicycle mixes with oxygen in the air. The reaction makes a new substance, rust.

Early cameras used a chemical reaction to make a flash.

BRING ON THE HEAT

- The bright flash of early flashbulbs results from magnesium igniting in carbon dioxide.
- When you digest your food, chemical reactions give off heat that makes your body warm.
- Water added to metallic sodium produces plain table salt, but also catches fire with the quick release of heat energy.

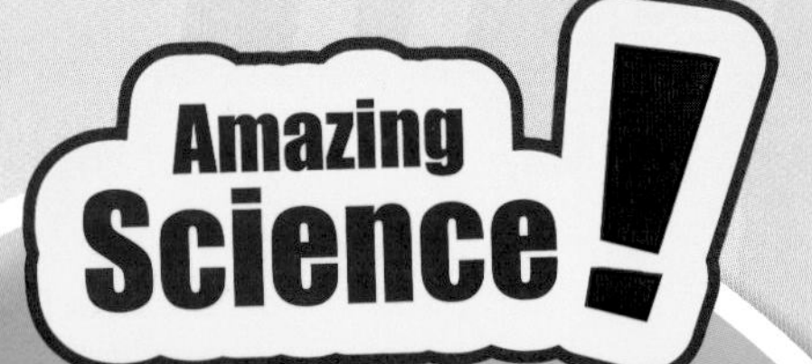

Alfred Nobel invented dynamite to help miners. He didn't know it would be a weapon. He used money from his invention to fund the Nobel Peace Prize.

Is It Magic?

Clean pennies . . . with chemistry? Chemical reactions can produce some surprising results!

you will need:

- a tarnished penny
- vinegar
- salt
- teaspoon or metric measuring spoon
- bowl

1 Fill the bowl ¼ full with vinegar.

2 Add 1 teaspoon (5 mL) of salt.

3 Add your penny.

4 Swirl the bowl to mix.

5 Set the bowl aside for five minutes. What happens?

Chemistry at Home

Why do onions make you cry? Onion cells contain the chemical sulfur. When you cut an onion, the cells are broken. A chemical reaction takes place when the sulfur compounds react with the moisture in your eyes to form sulfuric acid. Your brain doesn't want acid in your eyes. So it sends a signal to your tear ducts to make more tears to dilute the acid. You cry to protect your eyes.

THE SCIENCE BEHIND IT!

Pennies contain the metal copper. Copper becomes tarnished and dull over time. Tarnish forms when copper comes in contact with oxygen in the air. The reaction makes a substance called an oxide. When you put the penny in vinegar (acid acetic) and salt (sodium chloride), they combine to form hydrochloric acid. The acid removes the oxide. Without the oxide, you have a shiny penny again.

Funky Foam

Use materials around your house to make messy, funky foam. If you do the reaction in a bottle with a narrow opening, the foam will shoot out like a volcano.

You will need:

- lemon juice, orange juice or vinegar
- liquid dish soap
- baking soda
- tray
- tablespoon or metric measuring spoon
- 1 8-oz (237 mL) drinking glass
- spoon

1. Pour ¼ cup (59 mL) of lemon juice, orange juice or vinegar into a drinking glass.

2. Add 10 drops of dish soap to the liquid in the glass.

3. Place the glass on a large tray.

4. Add a heaping tablespoon (4 mL) of baking soda to the glass and stir.

Watch what happens!

Another Reaction at Home

Have you ever made invisible ink? Put lemon juice on a toothpick and write a "secret" message. When you want to read the message, hold the paper near a light bulb—but not close enough for the paper to catch fire! Soon, you'll see the message. Why? Lemon juice is an acid that weakens the paper. When you heat the paper, the part with the juice burns before the rest of the paper.

THE SCIENCE BEHIND IT!

You made a chemical reaction. Lemon juice, orange juice, and vinegar are all acids. When the acid comes in contact with the baking soda, a base (a chemical that reacts with an acid to form a gas called carbon dioxide), the two chemicals react to produce carbon dioxide gas. The mixture of carbon dioxide gas and liquid dish soap creates funky foam. Adding food coloring will make your foam even funkier. Just be careful not to spill the foam from the tray.

Dancing Pasta

Your spaghetti just sits on your plate, right? Actually, you can make it move. How? With chemistry.

you will need:

- 1 8-oz (237 mL) drinking glass
- a few pieces of cooked spaghetti or other long, thin pasta
- baking soda
- vinegar
- teaspoon

1. Put water in the drinking glass, almost to the top of the glass. Mix in a teaspoon of baking soda.

2. Add a teaspoon of vinegar. This should cause some "fizzing" in the glass.

3. Add a couple pieces of spaghetti. Watch closely to see what happens. How long will the spaghetti dance? Time it and see.

You can do the same experiment with raisins.

Amazing Science!

Acid-base chemistry can be delicious. The dark color of chocolate cake depends on how much base, such as baking soda, you add to the batter.

THE SCIENCE BEHIND IT!

Baking soda is the chemical sodium bicarbonate. It reacts with vinegar (acetic acid) to form carbon dioxide gas. This is the gas that you breathe out from your lungs. Carbon dioxide gas is released from the solution you made. It rises to the top of the glass in tiny bubbles. If there is something for the gas molecules to hang onto, like the spaghetti, they attach themselves to it. As more and more gas bubbles cling to the spaghetti, they cause it to rise to the top of the glass. When the bubbles reach the top of the glass, the gas is released into the room. The spaghetti sinks to the bottom, only to be picked up by more gas molecules.

THE FREEZING POINT

How Low Can You Go?

If you want to ice skate outside, you have to wait for the water to freeze. **Freezing point** is the temperature at which a liquid begins to turn into a solid. Water in a pond or lake starts to freeze at 0 °C.

Be careful! You should walk or skate only on ice that is frozen solid.

The temperature of the Arctic Ocean is well below 0°. Most of the year, the ocean is covered with sea ice.

How low does it go?

Water in the ocean is very different from pond water. Ocean water has salt in it. It is a mixture. The salt in saltwater lowers the freezing point, or temperature at which the water can freeze. This means that the temperature must go much lower—become much colder—for saltwater to freeze.

FREEZING POINT . . . AND SAFE DRIVING?

Have you ever wondered why road workers put salt on the street when it snows? Adding salt to the roads makes a sort of saltwater mixture with the melting snow. Like the salt water in the ocean, the salty snow has a lower freezing point. The temperature has to drop lower for the salt and melted snow to form ice on the road.

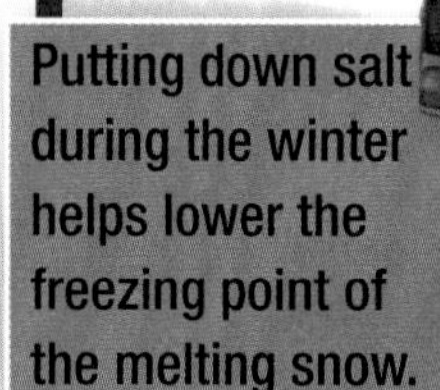

Putting down salt during the winter helps lower the freezing point of the melting snow.

Instant Ice Cream

In order to make ice cream, you need to bring the temperature of the cream or milk down to below 0°C.

you will need:

- milk, cream, or half & half (the higher the milk fat content, the richer your ice cream will be)
- vanilla extract or chocolate syrup
- sugar
- ice
- salt
- large and small self-sealing bags
- newspaper

1 Using a small self-sealing bag, add all the ingredients below:
one teaspoon (5 mL) of sugar
2 oz. (59 mL) of milk, cream, or half and half
a dash of vanilla extract or 1/2 teaspoon (2.5 mL) of chocolate syrup

2 Seal the bag and squeeze it to mix all of the ingredients well.

3 Fill the large bag about half full of ice. Add 1 cup (237 mL) of salt. Put the small bag into the large bag and seal everything securely.

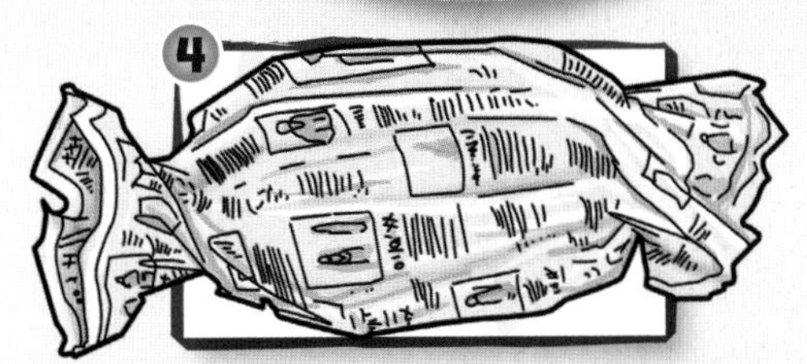

4 Using sheets of newspaper, wrap the bags and roll them into the shape of a tube. Tape the ends. Shake the entire bag for five to ten minutes.

5 After you have completed shaking the bags, open and enjoy your instant ice cream!

THE SCIENCE BEHIND IT!

This experiment involves something called "freezing point depression." Salt (its chemical name is sodium chloride) actually lowers the freezing point of water so that it freezes at a lower temperature. When you are making ice cream using ice and salt, this decrease in temperature allows the milk and sugar to freeze quickly to form ice cream. Freezing point depression is a really useful thing in cold climates. Salt is spread on roads and driveways to prevent ice from forming—and to melt it on cold days.

ACIDS AND BASES

Scientists have different ways to classify matter. Many substances can be classified as **acids** or **bases.** Lemon juice is a weak acid. Like lemon juice, most acids taste sour. Some strong acids can attack your skin and ruin your clothes. A base is the opposite of an acid. Soap is a weak base. Strong bases are just as dangerous as strong acids. That's why they might irritate your skin unless you wear rubber gloves.

IN THE SWIM OF PH!

The **pH** is important to keep a swimming pool clean and safe! The pH of our eyes is slightly basic, at 7.2. To keep a pool comfortable, the pH needs to be somewhere between 7.0 - 7.6. When the pool's pH is too low acidic water can dissolve the cement or marble side of the pool, creating places for algae to grow. Metals on the stairs and pumps could corrode, and your eyes and nose burn. If the pH gets too high, you can still have problems with itchy eyes and dry skin. Swimming pool water starts to get murky.

Having the correct pH makes this pool water sparkle!

What Is pH?

You can use **pH** to describe everything from shampoo to the water in a swimming pool. The value of pH is simply a way to measure how acidic or basic a liquid is. The value ranges from 0 to 14. Water is **neutral**—it's neither an acid nor a base. Acids have pH values between 0 and 7. What are the pH values of bases? You guessed it! From 7 to 14.

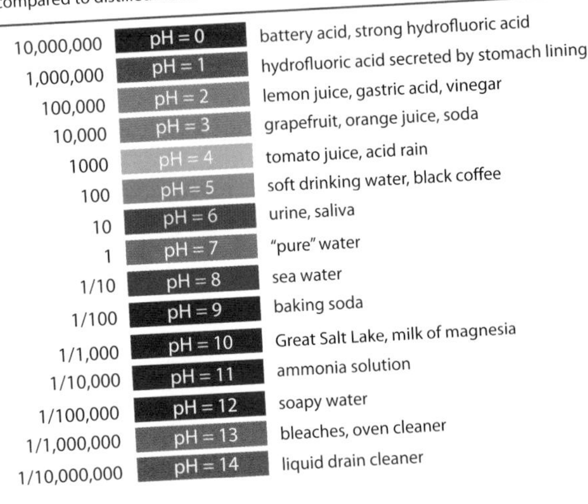

concentration of hydrogen ions compared to distilled water		examples of solutions of yhis pH
10,000,000	pH = 0	battery acid, strong hydrofluoric acid
1,000,000	pH = 1	hydrofluoric acid secreted by stomach lining
100,000	pH = 2	lemon juice, gastric acid, vinegar
10,000	pH = 3	grapefruit, orange juice, soda
1000	pH = 4	tomato juice, acid rain
100	pH = 5	soft drinking water, black coffee
10	pH = 6	urine, saliva
1	pH = 7	"pure" water
1/10	pH = 8	sea water
1/100	pH = 9	baking soda
1/1,000	pH = 10	Great Salt Lake, milk of magnesia
1/10,000	pH = 11	ammonia solution
1/100,000	pH = 12	soapy water
1/1,000,000	pH = 13	bleaches, oven cleaner
1/10,000,000	pH = 14	liquid drain cleaner

How Can You Tell an Acid from a Base?

Chemists use a pH indicator to decide if something is an acid or base. Make an indicator with things in your kitchen.

You will need:

- head of red cabbage
- medium-sized bowl
- grater
- strainer
- plastic container
- 4 clear plastic cups
- baking soda
- test liquids: lemon juice, vinegar, cola, milk

1 

Ask an adult to grate some red cabbage into a medium-sized bowl.

2 

Cover the cabbage with cold water. Let it sit for at least 45 minutes.

3 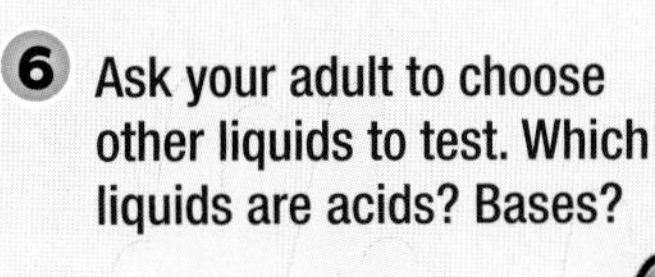

Carefully strain the juice into the plastic container. Now your indicator is ready to use.

4 

To test for acidity, pour an equal amount of juice into each cup.

5 

Put 1 teaspoon (5 mL) of baking soda into three of the cups. The fourth cup is the control that lets you compare your results. What color is the control liquid?

6 Ask your adult to choose other liquids to test. Which liquids are acids? Bases?

THE SCIENCE BEHIND IT!

The baking soda is a base. It will turn your cabbage juice blue. Test liquids to see how much you need to turn the cabbage juice to its original color. If you add an acid, the liquid becomes darker. The cup without the baking soda is your control. You'll want to get your mixtures to match that color. If you add a liquid and the juice stays blue, the liquid is probably not an acid. Red cabbage juice contains chemicals that cause the juice to change color when mixed with certain other chemicals. Add an acid to the cabbage juice, and it will turn different shades of red. Add a base, and the juice will turn different shades of blue.

How Can You Keep An Apple from Browning?

Believe it or not, acid-base chemistry can keep cut fruit and vegetables looking fresher.

You will need:

- an apple
- a potato
- a knife
- lemon juice

1 Ask an adult to help you cut an apple and a potato in half.

2 Put one half of both the apple and the potato aside.

3 Sprinkle lemon juice on the other half of the apple and potato.

4 Check your experiment after 20 minutes. Compare the two halves of the potato and apple. What do you notice?

THE SCIENCE BEHIND IT!

Some fruits and vegetables such as apples, pears, bananas, peaches, and potatoes contain an enzyme. When the fruit or vegetable is cut, the enzyme is exposed to air. The enzyme, oxygen, and iron in the plant create a chemical reaction that turns the cut portion brown. Adding lemon juice or another acid to the cut area will reduce the pH and slow the chemical reaction. However, the brown parts of fruit and vegetables are perfectly safe to eat.

Shocking? It's a Lemon!

Have you heard of battery acid? Lemon juice is an acid. You can use this acid to make a weak battery!

You will need:

- lemon
- small dish
- adult helper
- sharp knife
- 10 pieces of paper towel (1" x 2.5" or 2.5 cm x 6.4 cm)
- 5 pennies
- 5 dimes (or other coins that do not contain copper)

1 Have an adult helper cut the lemon in half. Squeeze the lemon juice into the small dish.

2 Soak all the paper towel strips in the lemon juice.

3 Make a tower with the coins. Alternate the dimes and pennies. Separate each coin with a juice-soaked piece of paper towel.

4 Moisten both your index fingers with water. Hold the tower of coins horizontally between your fingers. You will feel a small (and safe) tingle at your fingertips!

THE SCIENCE BEHIND IT!

You have just created a "wet-cell" battery! Electrons are conducted from one metal coin to the other through the lemon juice, producing a tiny electric shock at your fingertips. Today we use dry cell batteries instead of wet cell batteries. A dry cell battery is made up of 32 different kinds of metal, separated by blotting paper that has been soaked in a really strong acid and then dried.

The First Battery

Alessandro Volta created the first battery in 1800. He alternated layers of zinc and blotting paper soaked in salt water and silver. The top and the bottom layers needed to be made of different materials for the battery to work. By attaching a wire to the top and bottom of the pile, you can measure the voltage given off by the battery.

WAVES

Light, Sound, Energy!

Waves are part of your life every day. Sound waves, light waves, radio waves—did you know the world is full of waves?

Many waves travel through a medium. The medium could be air, water, or some other material. All waves carry energy from place to place. An ocean wave is actually moving energy, not water. The water happens to move because of the change in energy.

Ocean waves carry energy!

The Speed of . . .

Sound: The speed of sound traveling through air is approximately 1,115 feet (340 m) per second. Sound can actually travel more quickly through water than through air.

Light: In a vacuum, light travels at 984,251,969 feet (300,000,000 m) per second!

SOUND WAVES

Someone bangs on a drum. Do little pieces of "drum sound" travel to your ears? Of course not! Sound travels in waves. Sound waves need a medium to travel through. That means sound waves cannot travel in a **vacuum**. In this case, they travel from the drum through the air to your ear, where they cause your eardrums to vibrate. The vibration is what makes the sound.

LIGHT WAVES

Visible light waves are the only waves of light that we can see. We see the light waves as colors of the rainbow. Each color has a different wavelength.

How do we see? Our eyes have structures called **cones**. Cones receive tiny rays of visible light. When we see colors, we are seeing the color of light that is reflected off an object. When we see a red **flower**, we see red reflected from the flower. The other colors are absorbed by the flower.

Slinky™ Science

What does a Slinky™ have in common with the ocean? Both of them can make waves!

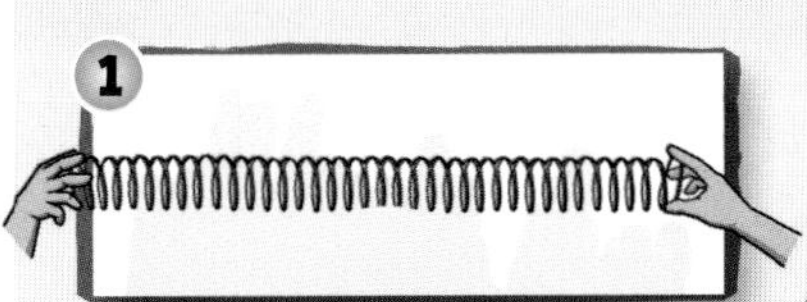

Hold one end of the Slinky™. Have a friend hold the other end.

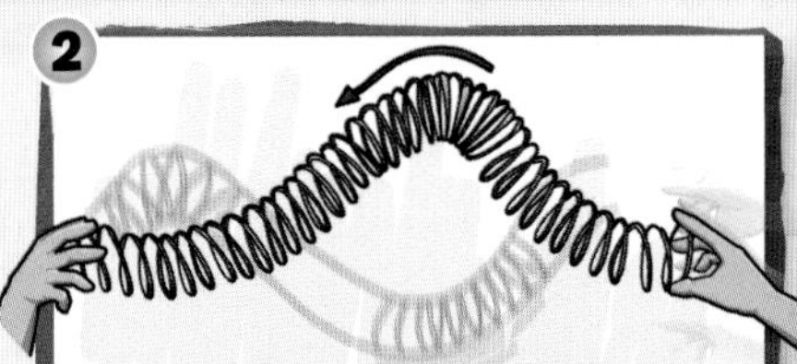

As your friend holds one end steady, move the other end up and down. This creates a **transverse wave.** Watch as the wave **reflects** off the stationary end, or the end your friend is holding. Try making the wave move more slowly or more quickly.

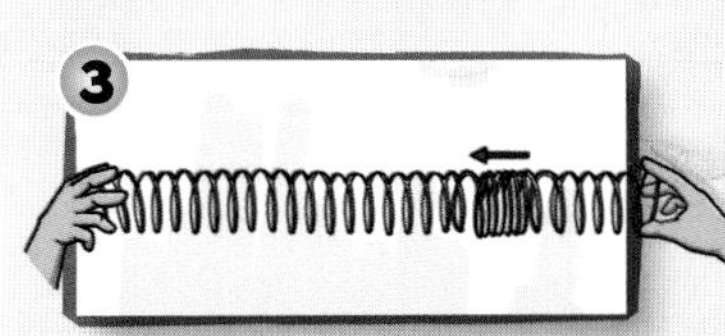

Now push your end toward your friend. This creates a longitudinal wave. This kind of wave can also reflect off the other end!

4 Make a transverse wave again. Keep moving the end up and down. Watch as the waves reflect.

See if you can see the crests (peaks) and troughs (valleys) in your standing wave.

THE SCIENCE BEHIND IT!

There are two types of waves—transverse and longitudinal. Because of the properties of the Slinky™, you can use it to model both types of waves. Which of the waves you made with your friend was transverse? Which was longitudinal?

Transverse wave: The medium moves perpendicular to the direction of the wave.

Longitudinal wave: The medium moves parallel to the direction of the wave.

Transverse

Longitudinal

THE SCIENCE OF SOUND

Are You Hearing Things?

Working around loud noises requires ear protection.

Your senses of smell and taste involve some kind of chemical reaction. There are no chemicals in your ears that make them hear. The ears are incredible organs! So, how do they work?

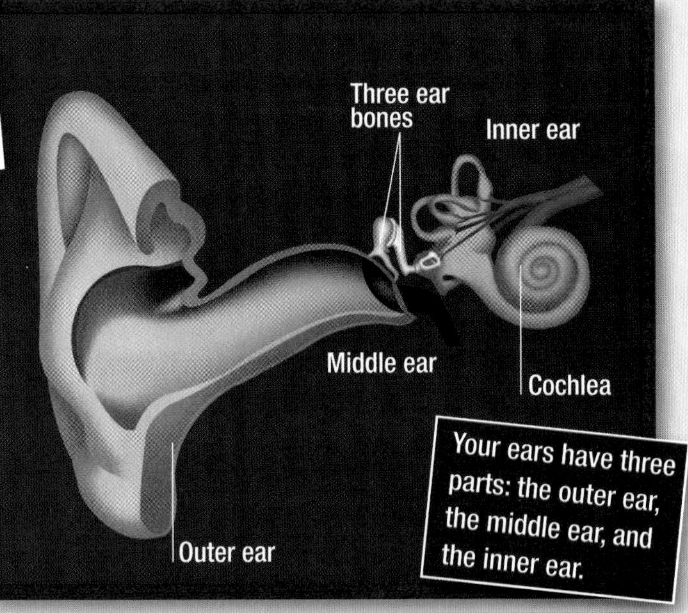

Your ears have three parts: the outer ear, the middle ear, and the inner ear.

OUTER EAR

This is the part of your ear you can see. Its main job is to collect sounds. The outer ear also has earwax. This sticky substance keeps dust and dirt from going any further into your ear.

What Is White Noise?

When all colors blend together, they create white light. Does it mean, then, that if all sounds blend together, they create white noise? The definition is very close! White noise is a combination of all the different frequencies of sound. A large fan makes a noise like white noise. White noise can block out other sounds. Your brain can only listen closely to one thing at a time. White noise has so many noises combined that your brain has to "tune out." That's why white noise might help you relax, focus, or even fall asleep.

MIDDLE EAR

Here's where the sound waves become vibrations. The sound waves hit the eardrum and then move along to smaller bones in the middle ear. Sound moves along to the inner ear.

INNER EAR

When the vibrations reach the inner ear, the sound comes to a small, curled tube called the **cochlea**. Tiny cells in the cochlea move and send **nerve** signals to the brain. Your brain understands these signals as sound. Turn up the radio!

Model Your Eardrum

How does your ear work? The eardrum is one important part of the process.

You will need:

- plastic wrap
- clear plastic cup
- elastic band powder
- uncooked rice (any other small grain will work)
- metal cookie sheet (or other noise maker)

1. Cut a small piece of plastic wrap and stretch it over the mouth of the plastic cup. This is your eardrum model.

2. Use an elastic band to secure the plastic to the cup. The plastic wrap needs to be stretched tightly so that it acts like a tight drum.

3. Spread about 20-30 grains of rice across the surface of the plastic wrap.

4. To see your model eardrum in action, use something like a metal cookie sheet or drum to make some noise. Hold the cookie sheet close to the cup. Strike the pan with a spoon to make a loud bang. What happens to the rice?

THE SCIENCE BEHIND IT!

Sound waves are made up of vibrations that travel through our ears. Your ear has an eardrum that is like a piece of very thin skin. This eardrum shakes when vibrations hit it. The shaking moves along a series of tiny bones and canals. The shaking eventually causes nerve signals to move to your brain. Your brain is the thing that figures out these nerve signals and interprets them as sound. Striking the pan creates sound waves. The sound waves travel to the plastic wrap and cause it to move. This moves the grains of rice.

HOW DOES LIGHT TRAVEL?

You flip on a light bulb in a dark room. What do you see? Light falls on objects in the room, even at a distance—and just from one light bulb! How does that light travel? Light travels in waves. A wave is traveling energy. Light waves are a type of energy that doesn't need a medium through which to travel.

A person who is colorblind may not be able to see the 25 in this picture.

A prism separates light into its wavelengths.

THE WAY WE SEE!

We call the light we see "visible light." But it's important to know the light that we classify as "visible light" is considered visible to humans! Dogs, for example, have a hard time telling the difference between red and green. Some insects can see colors that humans can't see! And even some humans don't see all the colors. Many men are affected by a **defect** in their eyes that causes **color-blindness**. Being color-blind doesn't mean you can't see any colors. It just means that you can't see some colors.

WHAT'S A LIGHT-YEAR?

Imagine trying to describe the distance between stars in the universe. They are so far apart, using miles or kilometers would make huge numbers! So scientists invented a new measure of distance: the **light-year**. A light-year is the total distance that a beam of light can travel in a year. A beam of light travels 186,411 mile/sec (300,000 km/sec), so the distance light travels in a year is a big number: 5.88 trillion miles (9.46 trillion km).

Why Is The Sky Blue

The sky looks blue because of light! This experiment will help you see the light.

You will need:

- a clear, straight-sided plastic drinking glass
- water
- milk
- measuring spoon
- flashlight
- white piece of cardstock paper

1

Fill the glass about 2/3 full of water.

2

Darken the room. Place the glass on one end of the paper. Shine the flashlight through the glass at the top of the water so that a shadow falls on the paper. Look at the edge of the shadow on the paper. What colors do you see?

3

Add ½ teaspoon (2.5 mL) of milk and stir.

4

Hold the flashlight so that light shines through the glass to the side. Look at the water. What color do you see?

5

Hold the flashlight so that light shines through the glass towards you. Look at the water. What color do you see?

THE SCIENCE BEHIND IT!

You are experimenting with light refraction. Light travels in straight lines. Its direction changes when it bounces on particles in the air. We say that the air or dust refracts, or bends, light. Different colors of light bend or refract in different ways. This depends on the wavelength of the light. Different colors of light are just electromagnetic waves with different wavelengths. How much the light bends depends on the wavelength of the light. The light of the colors of the rainbow have a different index of refraction in the same material. Your flashlight shines white light. The water refracts the white light into the colors of the rainbow. Adding milk to the water is like adding dust particles to the atmosphere. The light refracts more because of the tiny milk particles in the water. You see a blue color when the flashlight shines across the water — like seeing a blue sky. You see an orange-red color with the flashlight shines through the water at you — like seeing a sunrise or sunset.

It's Shocking STATIC ELECTRICITY

It's a chilly day, and you've worn a cap to keep your head warm. You take the cap off and your hair stands straight on end! What's going on? **Static electricity**!

Static electricity starts with **atoms**, the tiny building blocks of all matter. Atoms have **protons**, **neutrons**, and **electrons.** Protons have a positive charge, electrons have a negative charge, and neutrons have no charge at all. Usually, atoms have equal amounts of protons and electrons. But if you rub things together, electrons can move.

Static electricity looks shocking!

HOW MUCH SHOCK?

When your hair rubs a cap, it can stand straight up on end from static electricity. Which materials make the most static? Take a look at this list. The materials at the top make the most static electricity. The material at the bottom makes the least.

1. your hand (as long as it's dry!)
2. glass
3. your hair
4. nylon
5. wool
6. silk
7. paper
8. cotton
9. rubber

Have you ever been "shocked" touching a doorknob? Electrons move from the rug to you. You have extra electrons! So when you touch the doorknob, the electrons move to the doorknob. That's why you feel a zap!

Wool yarn makes some static electricity.

Shocking Science

You can create a little electricity with wool and a pie plate. Don't worry, though. The little shock in this experiment is harmless!

You will need:

- a Styrofoam™ dinner plate
- a Styrofoam™ cup
- a piece of wool cloth, like a scarf or sweater (Wool works the best, but you can try other fabrics, too.)
- an aluminum pie plate
- clear tape

1

Rub the Styrofoam™ plate with the wool cloth for a full minute.

2

Place this charged plate upside down on a table or the floor.

3

Tape the Styrofoam™ cup to the middle of the aluminum pie plate.

4 Place the pie plate on top of the charged Styrofoam™ plate using the cup as a handle. Bring your finger near the pie plate. You will feel a little shock and hear a "snap." If the room is dark, you should see a little spark.

When you rub the Styrofoam™ plate with a wool cloth, you charge it up. The Styrofoam™ attracts the electrons from the cloth when the two are rubbed together. The electrons cannot leave the pie plate, because it is completely surrounded by insulating air and Styrofoam™. If you touch the pie plate while it is near the Styrofoam™, the moving electrons will "jump" off the pan and onto you. That will cause you to feel a little shock, hear a snapping sound—and maybe even see a spark of electricity.

Can You Bend Water?

Turn on the faucet so that water comes out in a small stream, about 1/8" (3 mm) thick. Charge a plastic or rubber comb by running it several times through long, dry hair or rubbing it vigorously on a wool sweater. Slowly move the comb toward the water. What happens to the water?

LIQUID, SOLID, OR GAS?

Matter is anything that has mass and volume. All things are made of matter. But how can we classify matter? One way is to classify matter by its **state.** You can see some of the states in water. When you pour water into a pan, it's a liquid. Heat that water to boiling, and it becomes water vapor, which is a gas. Pour water into a tray and freeze it, and you have a solid. You still have the same substance with different properties. Water undergoes a **phase change**, not a chemical change.

Steam from geysers behaves like a gas.

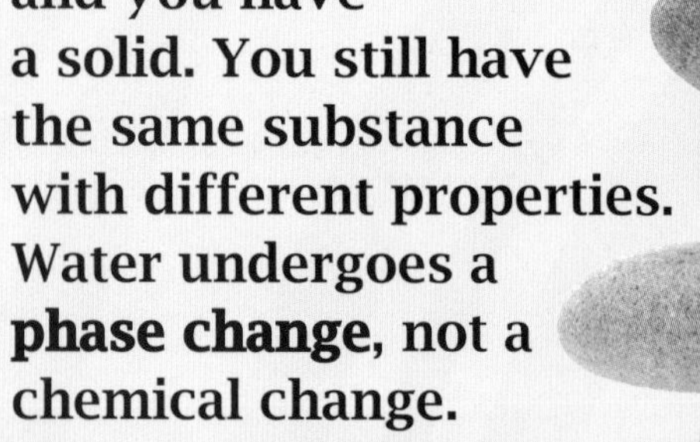

STATES OF MATTER

Each state of matter has its own properties:

- **Solid**: A solid has a definite volume, size, and shape that do not change at a given temperature. A rock at room temperature is a solid.
- **Gas**: The volume of a gas depends on the temperature and the pressure around the gas. Gas will take the shape of its container, but it will spread out into the surrounding area. You put helium into balloons to make them float. Helium is a gas.
- **Liquid**: A liquid has a definite volume, but it takes the shape of its container. Water is a liquid.

Plasma is one state of matter.

A FOURTH AND FIFTH STATE OF MATTER

At extremely high temperatures, matter can lose all of its electrons. This matter is called **plasma**. Plasma is air that's made by lightning and is found in stars, such as the Sun. Plasma is so full of energy, it takes on the consistency of sludge!

Changing States

Watch the state changes in a common substance—water!

You will need:

- a large plastic bowl
- plastic wrap
- a weight, such as a coin
- a smaller container, such as a yogurt container cut in half
- an elastic band or piece of string

1. Put the small container inside the large bowl.

2. Pour some water in the bowl. Do not let it reach the top of the small container.

3. Cover the bowl with plastic wrap. Secure it with the rubber band or string.

4. Set a weight on the center of the plastic wrap. Leave the bowl in a sunny spot for a few hours.

5. You should find the water in the small container is evaporating. Check the small container. Where did the water go?

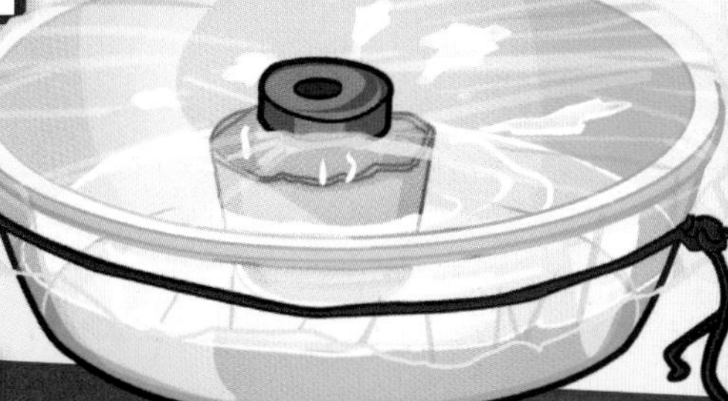

Juice Pops!

You can observe a change from liquid to solid—and enjoy a yummy treat!—by creating ice pops. Pour juice in paper cups. Place the cups in the freezer. Check after an hour or so. If the juice is slushy, place a wooden craft stick in the juice and place the cups back in the freezer. Once the juice is frozen solid, peel off the paper cups. Enjoy the solid ice pops!

THE SCIENCE BEHIND IT!

The heat of the Sun causes the water to evaporate. The water vapor rises and condenses on the plastic wrap. The condensation falls back into the container. The weight guides the condensation back down into the container. This is a small version of the Earth's water. What would happen if you put ice in the water? Try it and see!

It's a Bird! It's a Plane!

IT'S A PROJECTILE!

Have you ever thrown a ball to teammate? Tossed a snowball to start a friendly snowball fight with friends? You are demonstrating an important part of physical science. Each object you've thrown is a projectile. The path an object takes in the air is called its trajectory.

A football travels in a trajectory.

ALL IN THE CURVE

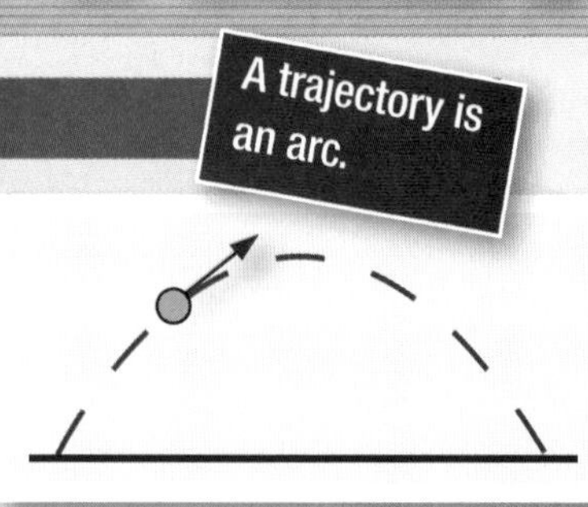
A trajectory is an arc.

When something travels through the air, such as a ball thrown to a teammate, it tries to travel in a straight line. But the trajectory of an object is a curve or **arc**. You can see this when you throw a pebble into a pond or lake. As the object leaves your hand, it travels in an arc until it splashes into the water. What brings the object back to Earth? Gravity!

TRAJECTORY VS. ORBIT

The terms *trajectory* and ***orbit*** both refer to the path of an object in space or air. *Trajectory* is used in connection with objects launched into the air that have a start and designated end point. For example, a ball thrown to a teammate has a start and end point. So too does a rocket that's shot to the Moon and is intended to come back to Earth. *Orbit*, on the other hand, is used in connection with natural bodies in space such as the planets or their moons. They do not have an end point. These are objects that continue to follow their paths, or orbits.

An orbit is a circular path.

Amazing Science!

There are approximately 2.5 million parts in a space shuttle — not including the astronauts.

Toy Around With Trajectory!

You will need:

- plastic spoon
- 3 cotton balls

A trajectory can be scientific fun. Use science to make a toy. Be sure you perform this experiment in a room with a lot of space. Do not aim projectiles at others!

1. Hold the spoon in one hand facing away from you.

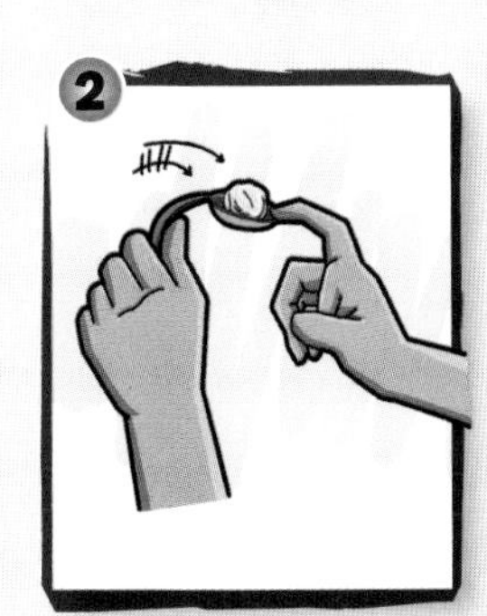

2. Place a cotton ball on the rounded part of the spoon.

3. Aim the cotton ball at an open area. Pull the top of the spoon back a little and release. Leave the cotton ball where it landed.

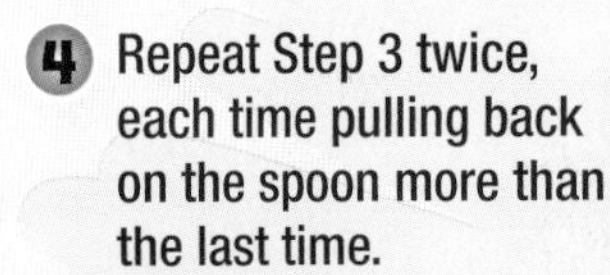

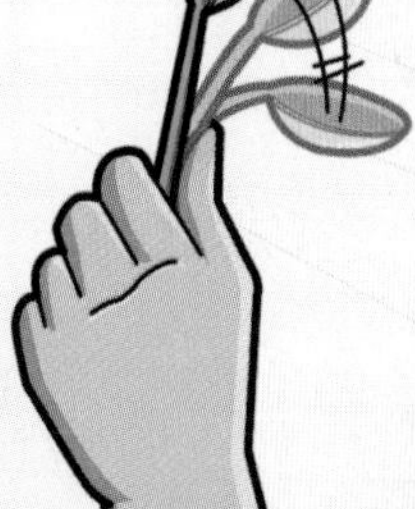

4. Repeat Step 3 twice, each time pulling back on the spoon more than the last time.

Catapult Away

Catapults were designed in ancient times as a weapon. A catapult launches an object over a great distance. Today, modern versions of catapults are used on aircraft carriers to launch fighter jets. Slingshots are also types of simple catapults. Catapults and slingshots launch objects with a great deal of speed, moving the object upward, and increasing the trajectory or distance the object travels.

THE SCIENCE BEHIND IT!

Your spoon is like a catapult and your ball a projectile. A projectile is an object thrown or dropped that continues in motion until stopped by the downward force of gravity. A catapult uses a lever. A lever is a bar that turns on a point called a fulcrum. Trajectory is the path of the projectile. You can change the trajectory of the projectile by changing the position of the fulcrum. You can do this by launching the ball from different angles. Changing the projectile's path will also affect where it lands.

SIMPLE MACHINES AND HOW THEY HELP US WORK

What do you think of when you hear the word machine? A washing machine? A bicycle? What about something as simple as a screw or a ramp? Believe it or not, all of these things are machines. Machines are tools that make it easier for us to do work.

A wheel and axle gets you ready to roll!

SIMPLE MACHINES

Simple machines are called "simple" because they have few or no moving parts. Think of a ramp used in a moving truck. A ramp does not have any moving parts. But it still helps people do work. Ramps are slanted surfaces that make it easier for heavy things to move from a lower place to a higher place or from a higher place to a lower place.

The ramp helps workers move a load over a distance.

SIX SIMPLE MACHINES

1. **Lever** A lever is a bar that pivots on a **fulcrum**. If you apply a force to one end of the lever, the other end lifts.
2. **Wheel and Axle** A wheel and axle consists of wheel attached to a bar, which changes the size of the force. A small force on the wheel makes a larger force turn the axle, such as in a doorknob.
3. **Pulley** A pulley is a simple machine made of a wheel with a grooved rim in which a pulled rope or chain can run. The pulley changes the force: When one end of the rope moves down, the other end of the rope moves up.
4. **Ramp** A ramp lets you use less force over a greater distance.
5. **Screw** A screw spreads a force over a distance. The threads in the screw allow the force to be distributed over a long distance.
6. **Wedge** A wedge changes a downward force to an outward force. A wedge has at least one slanting side ending in a sharp edge.

How Do Simple Machines Work?

If you have things to move from place to place, a wagon is a great tool made of simple machines!

You will need:

- shoe box
- wooden barbecue skewers, chopsticks, or other smooth or thin sticks
- small disposable paper or Styrofoam™ plates

1. Poke one skewer through the two long sides of your shoe box close to one short side to make your first axle.

2. Repeat with a second skewer on the other end of the box.

3. The skewer ends should stick out from the box. Make four wheels by attaching a plate to each end of each skewer.

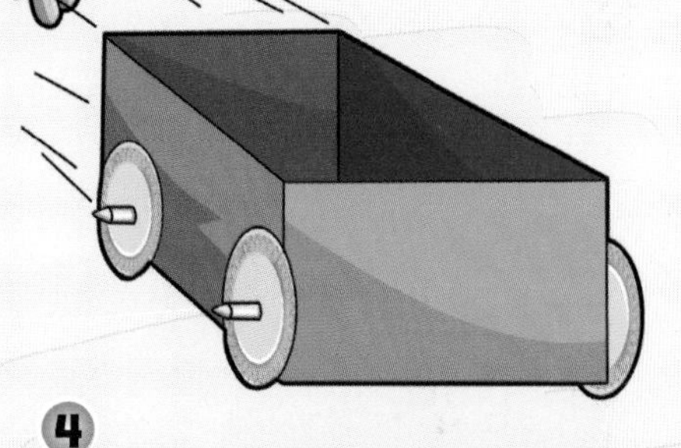

4. Push your wheel-and-axle wagon along the ground.

THE SCIENCE BEHIND IT!

The wheel and axle is a type of simple machine. Simple machines make work easier to do. If you try to push an ordinary box along the ground, the bottom of the box rubs against the ground, making it harder to push. This rubbing force is called friction. Pushing a box along the ground is much easier when you use a wheel and axle because there is less friction. Wheels and axles are used everywhere in modern life because they are so useful. How many devices can you think of that use this simple machine?

THE PRESSURE'S ON!

Air and Water Pressure

You're walking on a warm, sunny day. You can feel the sunshine on your skin, maybe a light breeze. Can you feel pressure pushing on you? Believe it or not, a huge amount of air is pressing on you! Why don't you get crushed from the pressure? Because our bodies have pressure that pushes outward. It all balances out.

You can't feel air pressure, but it's around you all the time!

HOW MUCH PRESSURE?

Air pressure is the force that is exerted on you (and other objects) by the weight of air molecules. You can't see the molecules, but they take up space and have weight. Air molecules don't naturally "pack in": there's space between them. So they can be pressed together to fit in a smaller space. Weather forecasters measure the pressure of large masses of air. If a lot of air is packed in a small space, that's a high-pressure system. High-pressure systems bring clear skies and cooler temperatures. Low-pressure systems bring warmer weather, but they can also bring rain and storms.

WATER PRESSURE

Water pressure is the force that is exerted on an object by the weight of water. Water is heavier than air, so water pressure is much greater than air pressure. The deeper that we go in water, the more pressure is exerted on our bodies. Water pressure is measured in units called **atmospheres.** For every 30 feet (9.1 m) or so that we dive down in the water, another atmosphere presses down on our bodies. We can only travel down to three or four atmospheres of pressure before we need the protection of a craft like a submarine.

Water pressure is greater than air pressure.

How Do They Do It?

The deepest place in the ocean is almost seven miles (11 km) deep! The water pressure there is more than 1,000 times greater than at sea level. How do the fish there keep from getting crushed? Their body tissue pushes back at the same pressure of the deep water. If these fish suddenly swam up thousands of feet, they could explode!

Deep Sea Diver

You can't send this submersible to the depths of the ocean, but you can still build a diving bell to watch water pressure at work.

you will need:

- a 2-liter plastic soda bottle
- 8 drinking straws (large milkshake straws will work best)
- a rock or other large weight
- masking tape
- string
- a bucket or sink to fill your container

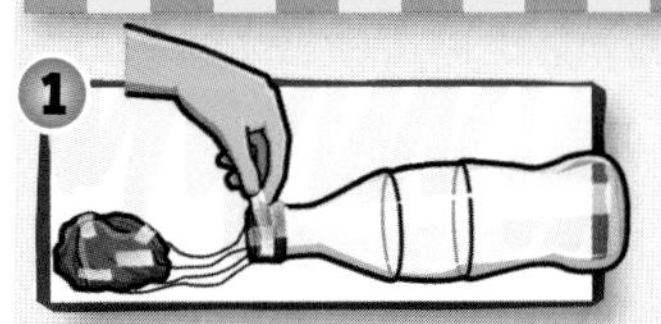

1. Tie a string around your rock (or weight). Then tie the other end of the string to the mouth of the container so that the rock hangs about an inch (2.5cm) directly below the center of the bottle opening. Secure the string to the opening with tape.

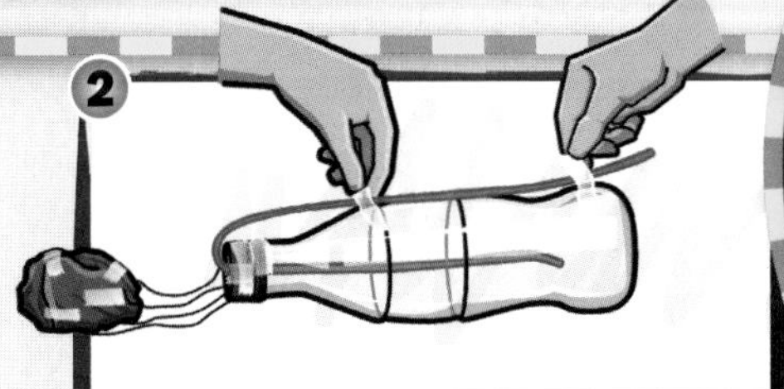

2. Create a long tube with your drinking straws by slipping them into the ends of each other. Insert one end of your tubing through the bottle opening all the way to the bottom. Then bend the tubing slightly, where it exits the container. Do not close the tube where it bends. Tape it to the outside of the bottle in two places: near the top and near the bottom.

3. Now fill your bucket or sink with water.

4. Block the end of the tube with your thumb and put the diving bell (your bottle) in the bucket or sink filled with water. The diving bell should float with the weight hanging down.

5. Now take your thumb off the end of the tube. The diving bell should sink. When the weight hits bottom, blow into the tube and it will rise again. See if you can get the bell to hover in mid-water.

THE SCIENCE BEHIND IT!

When you are scuba diving, the deeper you dive, the more water you have pushing against your body. Divers need to get air if they are going to work underwater for any length of time. One of the earliest inventions to do this was the diving bell, which trapped a supply of air for divers. A diving bell is connected to the surface by an air hose and cable and is weighted so it can overcome the pressure of the water to travel to the ocean bottom.

WHAT IS LIFE SCIENCE?

How do plants survive in places with little light? How many bones and muscles do our bodies have? How many kinds of insects live in the world? Why are some animals endangered? How is the desert different from the rain forest, the tundra, and the polar ice caps?

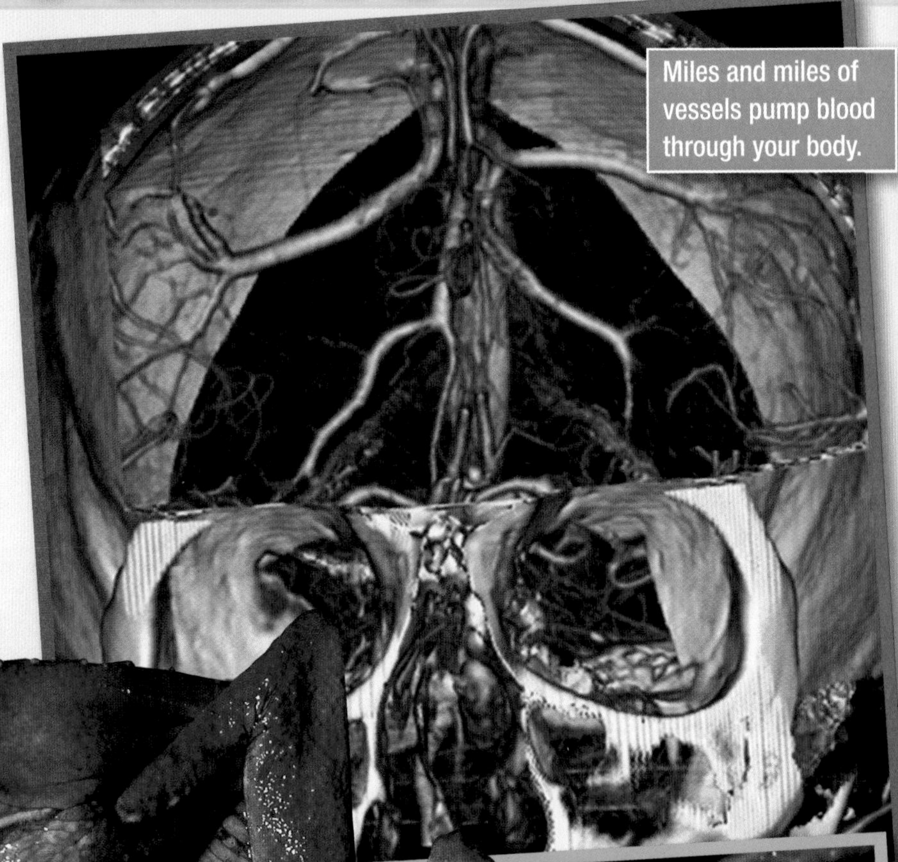

Miles and miles of vessels pump blood through your body.

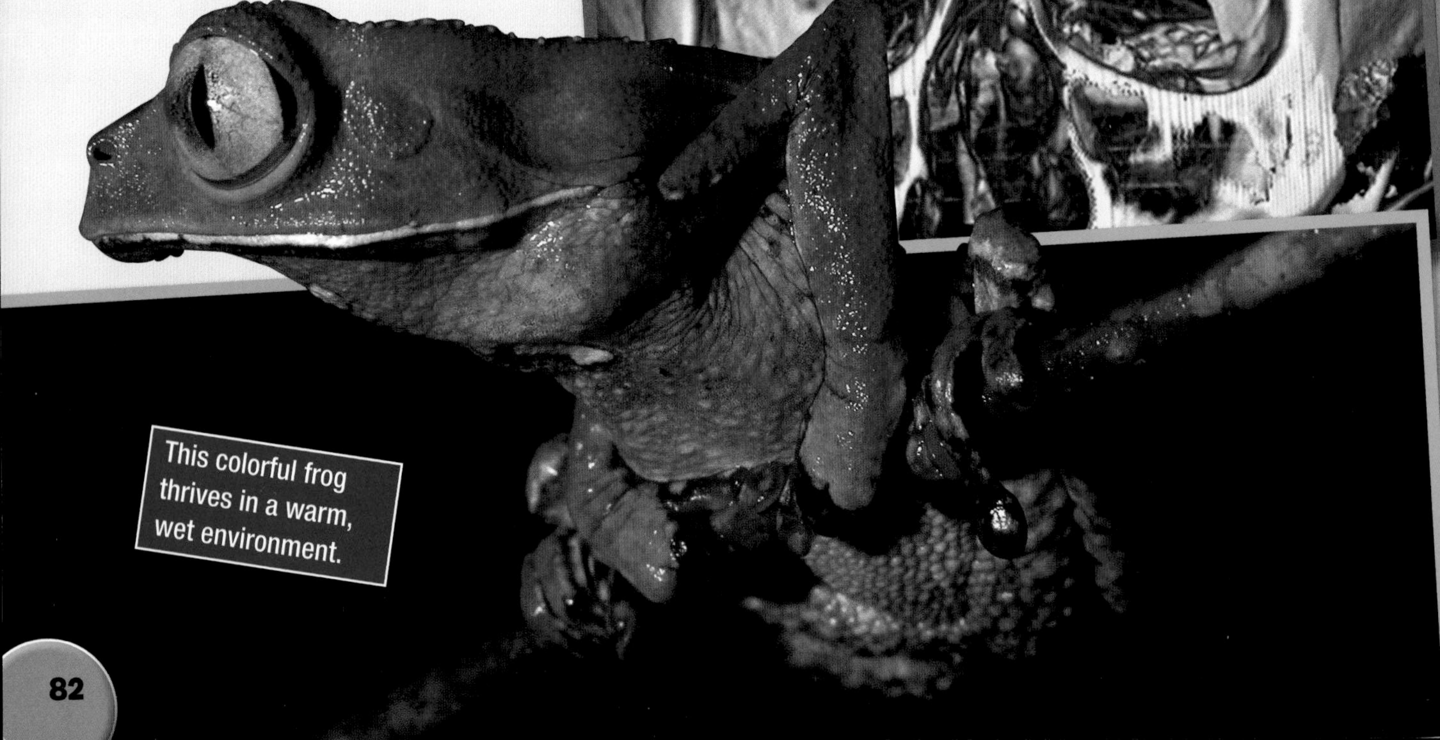

This colorful frog thrives in a warm, wet environment.

All these questions are part of a branch of science called **life science**. Life science is the study of living things— such as plants and animals. Life science explains how living things relate to one another and to their surroundings. In this part of the book, you'll find out more about plants and animals and how they manage to survive in the amazing places where they live. You'll learn about systems in our bodies that help us get the energy we need to move and grow. You'll study the way your heart works, classify animals, and get a closer look at cells! When you do the activities in this section, you'll have a window into the living world!

Some living things grow underwater.

Her muscles are at work!

Amazing Science!

- Did you know that if a spider damages one of its legs, it sheds it and grows a new one?
- The only bird that can fly backwards is the hummingbird.
- An adult anteater eats about 30,000 ants a day.
- Bats always turn left when they exit their caves.

A World Of ANIMALS

Scientists classify animals into groups. They ask questions to classify animals, such as, "What is the animal's body like? How does it get food? How does it reproduce?" Based on the answers to questions like these, scientists group animals by their similarities. Mammals, birds, reptiles, and amphibians are some of the better-known animal groups.

A cat is a mammal.

MAMMALS

Mammals are covered by some sort of hair. Most give birth to live young and feed them milk. There are some 5,400 species, or types, of mammals known today. The largest of all mammals actually lives in the oceans. It's the blue whale. And yes, whales *do* have hair!

BIRDS

Birds are covered with feathers and have wings. They lay eggs. There are about 10,000 living species of birds in the world. The ostrich is the largest of all birds. An ostrich egg is about the size of a large dinner plate.

REPTILES

A reptile's skin is covered in scales instead of hair or feathers. Reptiles need the warmth of the Sun to stay alive. They do not generate enough heat within their bodies. Ancient reptiles were known as the dinosaurs. But most of today's reptiles are much smaller compared to those giants.

AMPHIBIANS

Amphibians live both on land and in water. Most amphibians spend their young lives in water. As they grow, their gills turn into lungs. Then they move onto land. They live near water because they like to keep wet. The amphibian populations have decreased all around the world. Many species are now threatened or extinct.

How Do We Classify Animals?

If you don't have groups of animals around you, that doesn't mean you can't classify. Try it with shoes!

You will need:

- [ ] several shoes (many different kinds)

1. Collect several shoes from around the house. Take only one of each shoe.

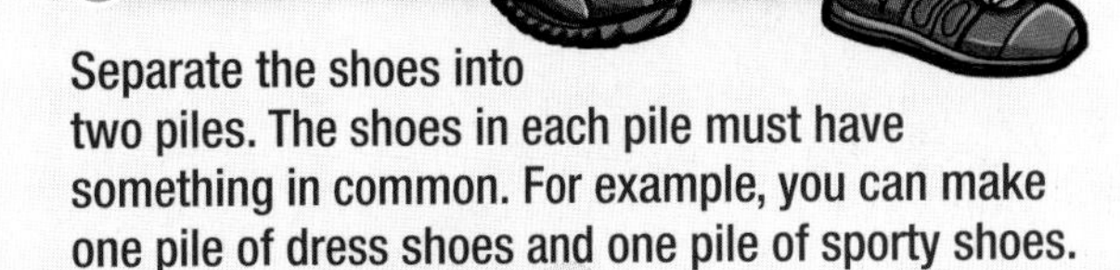

2. Separate the shoes into two piles. The shoes in each pile must have something in common. For example, you can make one pile of dress shoes and one pile of sporty shoes.

3. Look at the first pile of shoes. Separate that pile into at least two smaller piles. Each of the piles must have something in common, like color or heel size, for example.

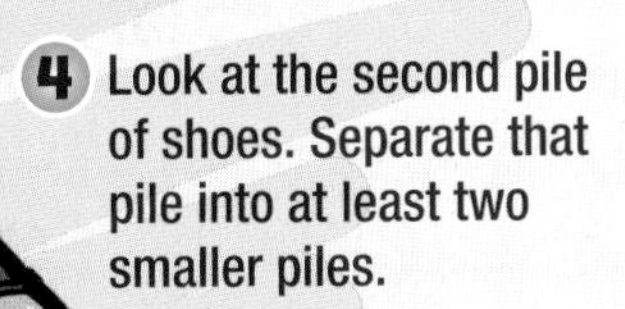

4. Look at the second pile of shoes. Separate that pile into at least two smaller piles.

THE SCIENCE BEHIND IT!

You just divided, or *classified* shoes into different categories. Scientists use classification as a way to organize information. The animal kingdom is divided into two large groups, vertebrates and invertebrates. Vertebrates are animals with backbones. These include fish, amphibians, reptiles, birds and mammals. Invertebrates are animals without backbones. These range from jellyfish, worms, crabs, and starfish to insects, spiders, and octopuses.

AMAZING ANIMALS

A chameleon's tongue is sticky and can stretch to be as long as the chameleon's body! Its tongue is an adaptation that helps the animal survive.

A sticky tongue comes in handy for catching food.

ANIMAL ADAPTATIONS

An adaptation is a trait that allows an animal to survive in its environment. Animals have special parts or ways of acting that allow them to survive. Opossums play dead to make **predators** leave them alone. Some lizards, such as certain kinds of skink, can drop their tails. When threatened, their tails fall off, allowing them to make a quick escape. Sharks have huge numbers of teeth that make them fierce **predators**. If their teeth break, they are quickly replaced by other teeth waiting in their jaws.

The platypus has many adaptations to help it survive.

Amazing Science!

Most animals don't eat moss. It's hard to digest and has little nutritional value. But reindeer fill up with moss. The moss contains a special chemical that helps a reindeer keep its body warm. When the reindeer makes its yearly journey across the icy Arctic region, the chemical keeps it from freezing.

A WONDERFUL AND WEIRD ANIMAL

A platypus has amazing adaptations. With its webbed feet, it's a mammal that is able to swim. One of the most interesting adaptations is how a platypus finds food underwater. A platypus shuts its eyes, ears, and nose. It uses **sensors** in its snout to pick up signals showing where the food is located.

Surviving the Cold!

Animals have to adapt to many different climates. How do they keep warm? Do this experiment to find out one way.

You will need:

- 3 resealable plastic bags
- ice cubes
- a friend

1

Take one of the resealable bags and close it most of the way. Blow into it so that it is full of air. Seal it quickly so the air does not escape.

2

Take another resealable bag and fill it with ice cubes.

3

Lay the bag filled with ice on your friend's hand. Leave it there for about 30 seconds. Ask your friend how it felt to have the ice on her hand.

4

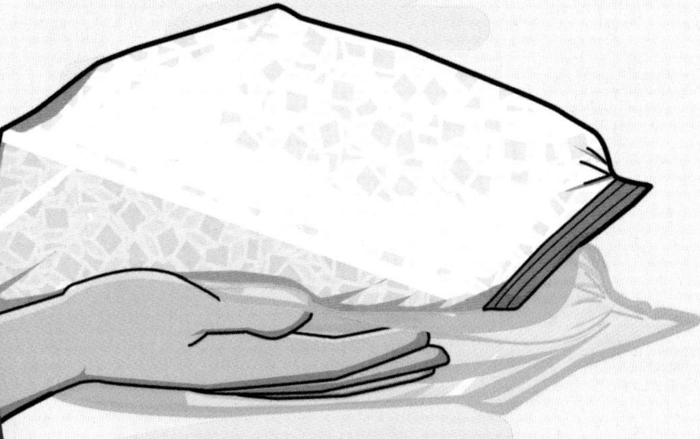

Now place the plastic bag filled with air on your friend's hand and then the bag filled with ice on top. Leave the bags for about 30 seconds. Ask your friend if her hand was colder or warmer than before.

THE SCIENCE BEHIND IT!

Did your friend's hand stay warm the second time? It should have. The layer of air between the hand and the ice cubes keeps skin warm. This illustrates how animals living in very cold temperatures are able to stay warm. In some cases, a layer of fat, represented by the bag of air, lies between the inner organs of an animal and its skin.

The Building Blocks of Life

CELLS

Cells are nature's building blocks.

All living things are made up of **cells**, the most basic unit of life. Different living things have different numbers of cells. An amoeba is an organism that has only one cell. A human body, on the other hand, has trillions of cells of different kinds.

DIFFERENT KINDS OF CELLS

There are different kinds of cells. In the human body, for example, there are many kinds of cells, each with particular jobs, such as nerve cells, fat cells, and blood cells. A collection of similar cells forms **tissue**. For example, bone cells in the human body make up bone tissue.

Bones are made of bone cells.

How are cells alike?

Nearly all cells have a nucleus. The nucleus "tells" the cell what to do. It is like the "brain" of the cell. Organelles are other parts of cells. Each organelle has a different job to do to keep the cell alive.

CELL SIZES

Cells are not all the same size. A chicken egg, for example, is large enough to see, even without magnification. Chicken eggs are huge compared to the cells that make up pollen or human skin. Bacteria cells, such as the cell that causes the strep throat, are even smaller.

Use a microscope to see cells close up.

What Do Cells Look Like?

Take a close-up look at your world.

- a magnifying glass
- three different types of paper
- leaves from three different types of plants
- a flashlight

1. Place one of the leaves on a table.

2. Hold the magnifying glass about ½-inch above the leaf.

3. Slowly move the magnifying glass closer to and farther away from the leaf until you see the leaf clearly through the lens. How does the leaf look?

4. Shine the flashlight on the leaf as you look through the magnifying glass. Do you see anything different?

5. Repeat the steps with the other leaves and the pieces of paper.

THE SCIENCE BEHIND IT!

You are using a scientific tool. The curved lenses on a magnifying glass make small things look big. Scientists use lenses to look closely at an object. Moving the magnifying glass closer to and farther away from an object changes how clearly you see. Scientists call this focusing the lens. Some lenses are very strong. The lenses in a microscope are strong enough to see cells. A cell is the smallest part of a living thing. You cannot see most cells with your magnifying glass, but you can see how cells fit together. The differences you see between the three leaves and the three sheets of paper are from the way their cells fit together. Shining light on the leaves and paper helps your eyes focus through the lens.

Get Moving

BONES AND MUSCLES

Imagine life without bones. Could you stand up? Could you walk? Without your bones and muscles, these movements would be impossible. Your body would be like a bag of skin! Why do you have bones? Your bones do two things. Some bones protect your body. Your rib cage, for example, keeps your heart and lungs safe from injury. Other bones give your body its structure. Your spine helps you stand up straight.

HOW DO BONES MOVE?

Hurdlers use bones and muscles to jump.

Your bones move, but they don't move by themselves. The muscles in your body pull on the bones and make them move. Your muscles are attached to your bones. When your body is preparing to move, your brain sends a signal to the muscles. The muscles contract, or squeeze together. When the muscles squeeze together, the bones attached to them move, too.

Your bones are living parts of your body. They grow, and they repair themselves when they break. Blood brings food and oxygen to bone cells. The blood also takes waste away.

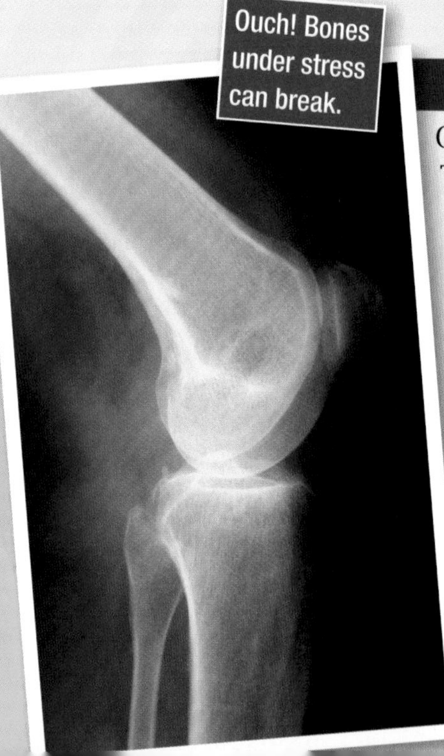
Ouch! Bones under stress can break.

A BAD BREAK

Ouch! Breaking a bone hurts. This X-ray shows a broken bone. Under a normal strain, bones will give a bit. But a sudden or strong pressure can snap a bone just like a pencil. If you think you have broken a bone, be careful not to move it too much until a doctor looks at it. Some breaks have to be fixed with surgery. Sometimes a cast can keep a bone steady enough to heal itself. Bones produce new cells to heal the bones and build them back up.

Rubbery Bones

This experiment should show you the importance of building your bones.

You will need:

- vinegar
- jar with lid
- an adult helper
- 2 chicken bones (Save the drumstick from your dinner!)

Safety Warning: Do NOT drink the vinegar or eat the bones. Everything should be thrown in the garbage when your experiment is over.

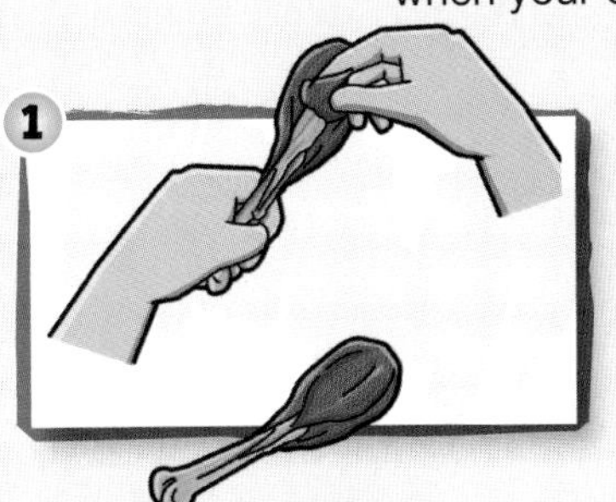

1. Ask an adult to help you take all the meat off the chicken bones.

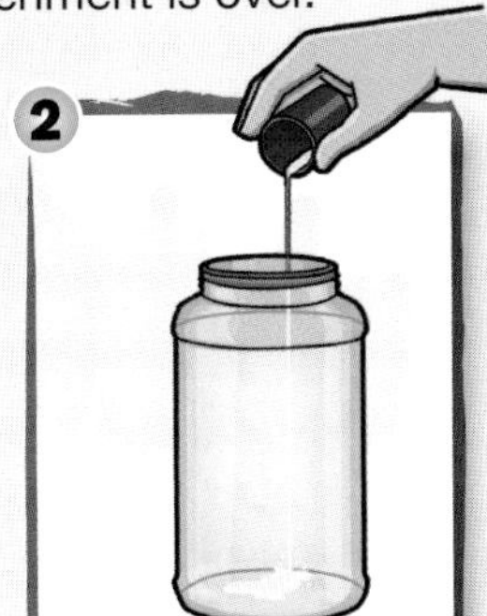

2. Fill the jar ¾ full with vinegar.

3. Place one of the bones into the vinegar. Put a lid on the jar and place it where it won't be disturbed. Allow it to sit for 24-48 hours.

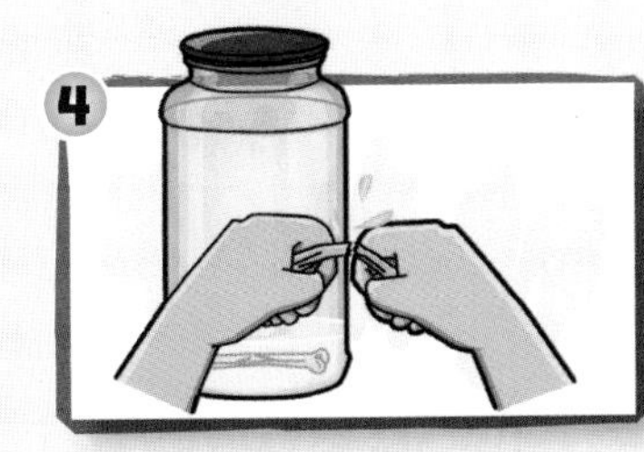

4. Examine the chicken bone that is not in the vinegar. Try to break it and look at the insides. Save this bone so you can compare it with the bone in the vinegar.

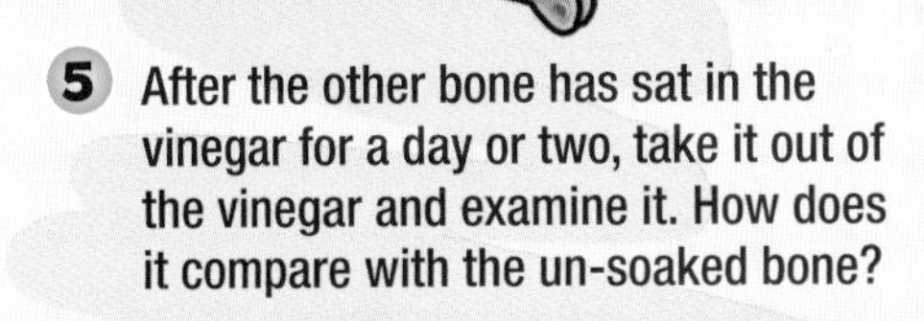

5. After the other bone has sat in the vinegar for a day or two, take it out of the vinegar and examine it. How does it compare with the un-soaked bone?

Bones by the Numbers

- When you were born, you had over 300 bones. As you grew, some of the bones fused together. An adult has far fewer bones than a baby—206 in all!
- Over 95% of the animals in the world do not have backbones. Most have rib cages, skulls, and jawbones, though.

THE SCIENCE BEHIND IT!

If we do not get enough calcium from the foods we eat, our bones can become very weak. Calcium is a mineral that helps keep our bones strong. The chicken bone that was soaked in the vinegar lost some of its strength because an acid in vinegar broke down the calcium. The vinegar dissolved the calcium, and the bone structure changed. This process can happen in our bodies if we do not get enough calcium.

THE DIGESTIVE SYSTEM

Food for Thought

These healthy foods are great for your digestive system.

You wake up in the morning. Then you eat a banana and a bowl of cereal before heading off to school. Besides tasting good, why do you eat? To supply energy and nutrients to your body. The digestive system is your body's way of turning the food you eat into something useful: energy.

WHY DOES MY STOMACH GROWL?

I'm hungry! My **stomach** is making embarrassing noises. Why? If you haven't eaten for a while, your digestive system releases some substances to your brain. These substances are a signal that says, "We need to eat!" Whether you eat or not, your brain sends a message to your digestive system to get ready for food. Your muscles move, and the fluids in your stomach get ready for food. That causes your stomach to "growl."

WHAT HAPPENS TO MY FOOD?

How does your digestive system work? Let's look at what happens to the food:

- **Take a bite.** As you chew, your digestive system is already hard at work. Your teeth grind the food. The saliva in your mouth starts breaking the food down. Your tongue pushes the food back to your throat.
- **The esophagus** is a tube that travels from the back of your throat down to your stomach. Your food is squeezed down the tube.
- **The stomach** is like a pink bag full of chemicals. The chemicals break down the food into little pieces.
- **The small intestine** is the next step after the stomach. The small intestine has **villi** (VIL eye). The villi absorb the nutrients in the food that you eat. Those nutrients move into the bloodstream to the different parts of your body.
- After the small intestine, the parts of the food that are still left enter the **large intestine.** There, the water in the food is squeezed out and sent back to your body. At the end of the large intestine, any leftover waste leaves your body.

Examine Your Taste Buds!

Are you a super taster? Do this simple test to find out.

- wax paper
- hole punch
- blue food coloring
- cotton swabs
- flashlight
- optional: magnifying glass

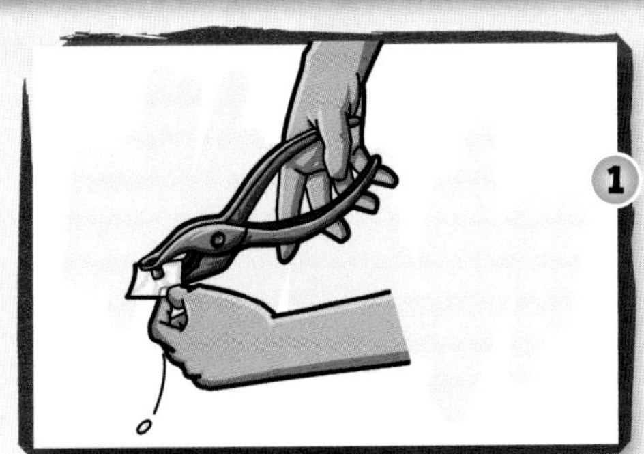

1. Using the hole punch, make a hole in the wax paper.

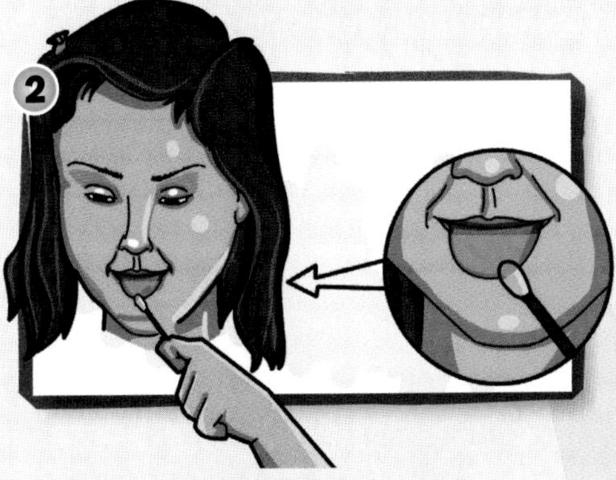

2. Using a cotton swab, paint a small section of the front of your tongue with the blue food coloring.

3. Place the hole in the wax paper on your tongue. You should see an area that you colored blue.

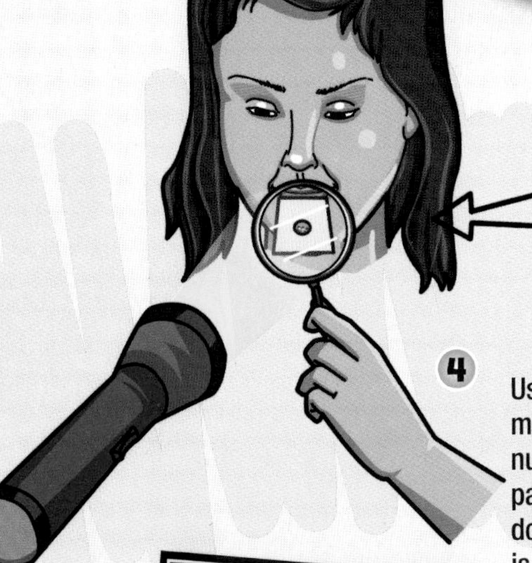

4. Use the flashlight and the magnifying glass. Count the number of pink, unstained (the part that is not stained blue) dots that lie in the circle. This is easier to do with a friend!

THE SCIENCE BEHIND IT!

Not all tasters are equal. Some people are actually "super" tasters. Each of us inherits our ability to taste. Some of us taste flavors better than others. This experiment allows you to count the number of taste receptors that you have in the wax paper circle. The unstained circles contain taste buds, or receptors. The more circles you count, the stronger that flavors will taste to you. This may be why one person doesn't care for a particular food while someone else thinks it's delicious. A super taster may have 25 dots or more in the wax paper section. If you are not a strong taster, you will have very few dots.

The Cardiovascular System
PUMP IT UP

A body's blood vessels and heart make up the **cardiovascular system**. The system moves blood through the body. Once blood leaves the heart, it travels through the body's blood vessels to the lungs. Here, the blood picks up oxygen needed by the rest of the body. The blood travels around the body releasing oxygen. In exchange, the blood takes away the waste—carbon dioxide. The cycle starts over again with the blood going back to the heart.

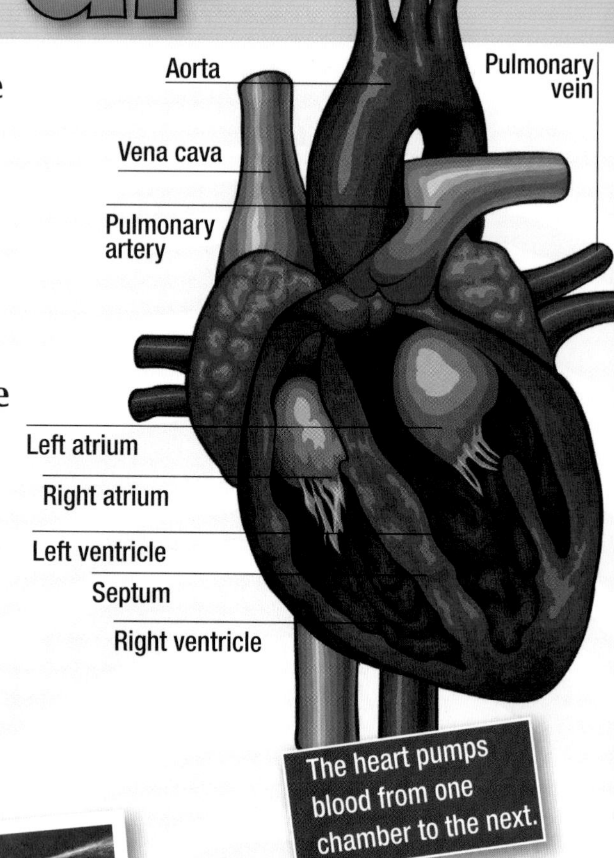

The heart pumps blood from one chamber to the next.

TRANSPORTATION TUBES OF THE BODY

The body consists of three major types of blood vessels. Arteries carry blood away from the heart. This blood is usually rich with oxygen. Veins carry blood toward the heart. Capillaries connect networks of arteries to the veins. It is in these tiny tubes that oxygen and carbon dioxide are exchanged within the blood.

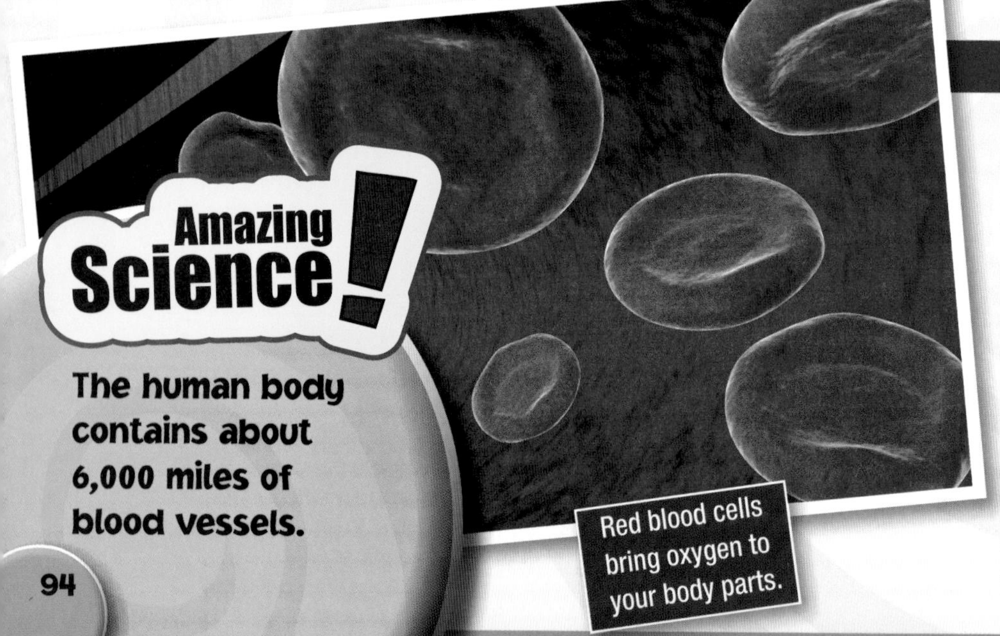
Red blood cells bring oxygen to your body parts.

Amazing Science!

The human body contains about 6,000 miles of blood vessels.

THE CIRCULATORY SYSTEM

Your heart is a muscle about the same size as your clenched fist. Clench your fist! The heart moves like your fist. Squeeze, relax, squeeze, relax . . . 70 times or so a minute at rest, even more if you are exercising. Can you hear your heart beat? That is the sound of the valves in your heart closing when they push blood through the chambers of the heart.

Pump It Up!

How hard does your heart really work? This experiment might give you an idea.

- 2 large pots, one filled with water
- watch or clock
- 1 towel
- an adult helper
- 1 plastic container that holds about 2/3 of a cup of liquid

1

Place both pots on a table and prepare to race your heart.

2

Use the cup to scoop water from one pot to the other. Have a friend time you. Try to scoop at least 70 times per minute.

3

See how long you can keep going at this rate! If you run out of water, start scooping back into the first pot again.

4

Wipe up spilled water with the towel.

THE SCIENCE BEHIND IT!

Could you scoop 70 scoops per minute? That's the same speed as a regular heart rate! The average adult heart pumps about 2/3 cup (150 milliliters or 5 fluid ounces) of blood into the arteries between 60 and 80 times every minute. That's at least one scoop per second! Your arm muscles get tired when they work as hard as your heart muscle does all the time. The special muscle your heart is made of is called *cardiac* muscle. It can keep pumping for your whole lifetime without getting tired.

Take a Deep Breath

YOUR RESPIRATORY SYSTEM

Every breath that you take brings precious oxygen into your body. Oxygen helps your cells move, reproduce, and turn food into energy.

Take a deep breath before you dive underwater.

THE DIAPHRAGM

The **diaphragm** is a muscle located right under your lungs. When you take in a deep breath, the diaphragm pulls down to make more space for your lungs to breathe air in. Your nose is part of the process, too. When you breathe in, air travels down the windpipe to your lungs. Once there, the air travels into tubes in your lungs called bronchi (BRON keye). The bronchi break into even smaller tubes. At the end of each tube is a tiny sac. Oxygen moves across the sacs' walls into the bloodstream.. They exchange the oxygen for materials your body doesn't use, like carbon dioxide. The carbon dioxide leaves your lungs when you exhale.

Air moves through bronchi, tubes, and sacs in the lungs.

Amazing Science!

The surface area of one human lung is equal to the area of a tennis court.

LUNG DISEASES

Your body automatically breathes. But some diseases can affect the body's ability to breathe. In **asthma**, the bronchi constrict. This cuts down on the flow of air. The respiratory muscles have to work harder to breathe. One out of every 12 kids in the United States has asthma. Many of these kids sometimes need medicine to help them breathe.

How Much Can You Breathe?

How much air do you think is in a breath? Here's a way to find out.

You will need:

- 1- or 2-liter plastic bottle
- 5-gallon or 15 L bucket
- water
- plastic tubing (or straws linked together)
- permanent marker

1 Do this experiment in a kitchen sink. Fill your bucket with water. Submerge the bottle so that it fills with water.

2 Hold your hand over the top to hold in the water as you turn the bottle back into the bucket upside-down.

3 Ask an adult or friend to hold the bottle in the bucket so that no water comes out of it.

Place one end of the tubing into the bucket and up into the bottle.

4 Take a deep breath and blow into the plastic tubing until you cannot possibly exhale any more.

5 Using the permanent marker, mark where the air and the water meet on the bottle.

Your friends can try the experiment, too.

THE SCIENCE BEHIND IT!

Air takes up space—this is the science that you used to measure the air capacity of your lungs. The average 4½-foot (1.4 m) child has a lung capacity of approximately two quarts (two liters). If you have a large lung capacity, you may be good at endurance sports, like cross country running, skiing, or distance swimming.

The Incredible NERVOUS SYSTEM

You can run and jump. You can do math problems. You even breathe while you sleep. How does your body know how to do all these things? Your nervous system controls your movements and much more.

PARTS OF THE NERVOUS SYSTEM

The **nervous system** has three parts: **brain**, **spinal cord**, and **nerves**. Your brain is the command center of the nervous system. It controls just about everything in your body. The spinal cord connects your brain to the rest of the body. It is your main link, taking messages to and from your brain. Nerves are either **sensory nerves** or **motor nerves**. Sensory nerves carry messages to the brain, such as what you hear or feel. Motor nerves carry messages from the brain to the rest of the body. For example, when you want to move your hand, your brain sends a message through your motor nerves for you to move your hand. It happens so quickly, you don't even think about it!

Nerves are located all over your body.

The brain is the control center for the nervous system.

THE BRAIN BOSS

The brain controls just about everything your body does, even when you are sleeping. The brain has five parts. The cerebrum is the biggest part of the brain. It is the part you use to think and to move your muscles. The cerebellum controls balance, and coordination. You can stand and balance because of the cerebellum. The brain stem connects the brain and the spinal cord. The pituitary gland is only the size of a pea, but it controls your body's growth. Finally, the hypothalamus controls your body's temperature.

Don't Be Nervous

Trick your knee with nervous system know-how.

- 1 helper
- 1 chair

1 Sit in a chair and cross one leg over the other.

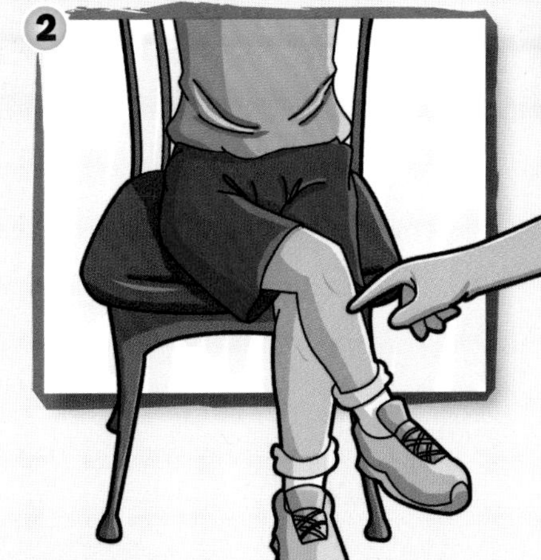

2 Find the dip in your knee just below your kneecap.

3 Ask your helper to tap the dip in your knee with the side of their hand, like a very gentle Karate chop.

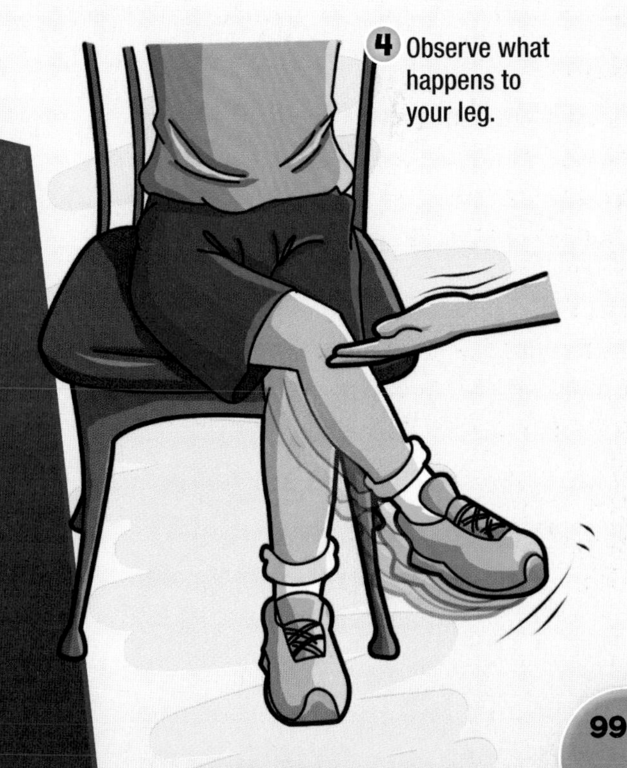

4 Observe what happens to your leg.

THE SCIENCE BEHIND IT!

Signals flow between your body, spinal cord, and brain in nerve pathways. Usually, your body sends messages to your brain, which then sends back a response. If your feet are too cold, for example, a message is sent to your brain, you realize your feet feel cold, and you may decide to put on socks. Sometimes, to protect you, your muscles and spinal cord can work faster in **reflex** actions. Tapping the dip in your knee causes a *knee-jerk reflex reaction*, and your leg kicks up like it has a mind of its own. This reflex protects you from falling down. If you are standing and the **tendon** in your knee suddenly gets longer, it means you are about to fall. The knee-jerk reaction quickly sends a message back from your spinal cord to straighten your leg to keep you standing.

What Do Plants Need to SURVIVE?

From a spiny cactus to a feathery fern, nearly all plants need the same things to live.

PLANT PARTS

What are the parts of a plant?

The **flower** often smells sweet to attract insects. Insects help plants reproduce. On some plants, flowers turn into fruit.

In a green plant, the **leaves** make food for the plant by taking in sunlight, water, and air.

The **stem** carries water to the leaves and flowers. The stem lets the plant grow toward the Sun.

The **roots** get water and nutrients from the soil. Roots also keep the plant steady in the ground.

PHOTOSYNTHESIS

Plants release oxygen in a process called **photosynthesis** (foh-toh-SIN-thuh-sis). In photosynthesis, plants capture energy from the Sun and combine that energy with carbon dioxide (a gas in the air) and water from the soil. Photosynthesis makes food for the plant in the form of sugar and starch. The plant releases oxygen into the air.

Even unusual plants need the same things as common ones!

What do all plants need?

Did you know that one tree can filter up to 60 pounds (27 kg) of pollutants from the air each year?

Do Plants "Sweat"?

When people are warm, they perspire. Some plants seem to perspire, too. Are they really sweating? Check it out!

You will need:

- 2 healthy broad leaves with long stems (peace lily or pothos)
- 2 wide-mouth jars or glasses
- 2 clear plastic cups, larger than the leaves
- 2 pieces of cardboard
- 2 small rocks
- food coloring
- petroleum jelly
- 2 cotton balls
- scissors

1. Have an adult hold the plant stems underwater and trim the stems diagonally with the scissors.

2. Fill both jars with water, and add 10 drops of food coloring in each jar.

3. Poke a small hole in the middle of each piece of cardboard. The hole should be just large enough to insert the stem of one leaf.

4. Cover the underside of one leaf with petroleum jelly. Insert a stem of a leaf through each hole. Seal the hole with a small amount of petroleum jelly.

5. Place the cardboard on top of each jar so that the stems are immersed in water. Place plastic cups over each leaf. Both leaves must be completely contained inside each cup.

6. Put a small weight on top of each cup and place the jars on a sunny window sill. Wait one hour and look inside the plastic cups.

Which cup contains moisture? Use the cotton balls to wipe the moisture in the cup. What color is the moisture?

THE SCIENCE BEHIND IT!

The moisture in the cup is from a process called transpiration. Transpiration happens when plants give off water vapor through tiny pores in their leaves, called stomata. Plants take in water from soil. The Sun's heat evaporates water from the leaves. As this water evaporates, more water is pulled through the stems and into the leaves again. In the experiment, one leaf absorbed the colored water and transpired the water from its stomata. The leaf that was coated in petroleum jelly could not transpire, because its stomata were blocked.

Where in the World Are BIOMES?

Think of a desert. What do you see? Maybe you see palm trees, sand, and wind storms blowing dry air around camels. Imagine a forest, with its leafy trees and creatures like squirrels and deer. Deserts and forests are two types of biomes.

Camels survive in the desert biome.

Forests have many types of trees.

The tundra is very cold.

BIOMES OF THE WORLD

Deserts cover about one-fifth of the world's land surface. Deserts are areas that are dry because they receive little to no rainfall. Not all deserts are hot. There are both hot and cold desert regions.

Forests cover about one-third of Earth's land area. You'll find different kinds of trees in forests. Tropical rainforests, deciduous forests, and evergreen forests are the major types of forests.

Grasslands have few trees.

Grasslands are like prairies. Although grass grows everywhere as far as you can see, very few trees dot this landscape.

The tundra biome is characterized by its extreme cold. Tundra biomes have very few plants or other types of vegetation. The Arctic tundra is near the North Pole. You'll find the Alpine tundra at the tops of snow-covered mountains.

Have you walked along a sandy shore or looked for tadpoles in a nearby stream? You have visited **aquatic** biomes, areas covered by water. Oceans, lakes, rivers, and ponds are all aquatic biomes.

What in the World Is a Biome?

If you can't visit the savannah or rainforest, you can observe a model of a biome in a bag.

You will need:

- clear plastic cup
- gravel
- soil
- grass seeds
- sharpened pencil
- water
- resealable sandwich bag

1 Fill the cup ¼ full of gravel.

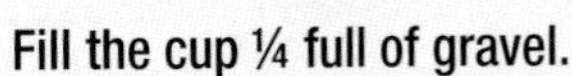

2 Add enough soil on top of the gravel so that the cup is ¾ full.

3 Sprinkle a few seeds on top of the soil. Use the tip of a pencil to push the seeds under the surface of the soil. Cover the holes with soil.

4 Add enough water to fill the gravel section of the cup.

5 Put the cup inside the bag and seal it.

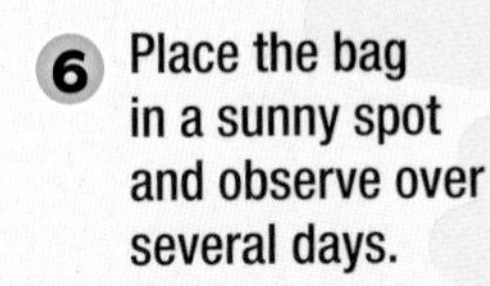

6 Place the bag in a sunny spot and observe over several days.

Aquatic Biomes

Some scientists classify aquatic biomes into two groups: saltwater biomes and freshwater biomes. Saltwater biomes are the world's oceans. Freshwater biomes are lakes, ponds, rivers, and streams. Most of the fresh water on Earth is frozen in polar ice and glaciers. That doesn't leave much water to drink!

THE SCIENCE BEHIND IT!

You created a mini biome. A biome is a large area that's set apart because of its weather conditions and the types of plants and animals that live there. This model biome needs a moderate amount of water and sunlight. There may be worms or other small insects living in the soil. The conditions were right to grow the grass. What can your model tell you about real biomes?

ECOSYSTEMS

Their Own Little Worlds

A biome is a large area that has similar plants and animals, such as the tropical rainforest or the tundra. So what is an ecosystem? An ecosystem is smaller than a biome—it could be as large as the Sahara Desert or as small as a backyard pond. An ecosystem is the interaction between plants, animals, and the nonliving things that work together. Each part of an ecosystem has its own role to play. Here are just a few ways in which parts of an ecosystem work together.

This bird will build its nest with plant material.

PLANTS PROVIDE SHELTER

Have you ever seen a bird's nest? Birds and most other animals use different plant parts for shelter. A bird uses twigs and leaves to build a nest. Twigs and leaves are different plant parts. Have you ever seen a house that is under construction? People use wood to build the frame of their homes. Lumber is a product from trees. Can you think of other ways people and other animals use plants for shelter?

Seeds can move from place to place tangled in an animal's fur.

ANIMALS MOVE SEEDS

We all know that plants can't get up and replant themselves in new spots. But plant seeds are scattered and grow in new places all the time. Animals help by scattering seeds. Animals move seeds in different ways. Some seeds stick to their fur. Some animals carry and move seeds in their mouths. When animals eat seeds, the seeds eventually pass through the animal and are dropped in different areas.

They Get Around!

How do animals help plants grow? Make a model . . . and take a walk.

You will need:

- 1 large fuzzy sock

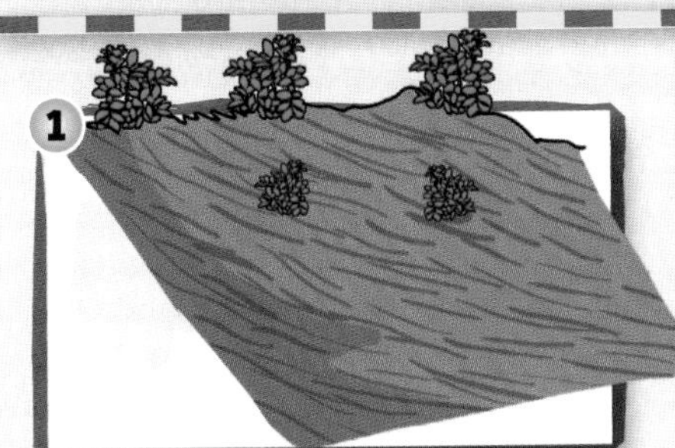

1. Find a grassy area, field, or nature center you can walk through. If you can, choose an area with lots of seed-bearing plants.

2. Put the sock on over one of your shoes.

3. Go for a walk through the area.

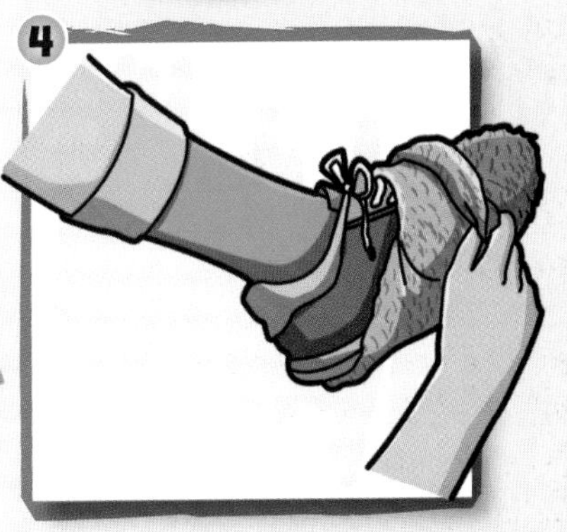

4. When you finish your walk, remove the sock and turn it inside out. Keep everything you collected during your experiment until you get home.

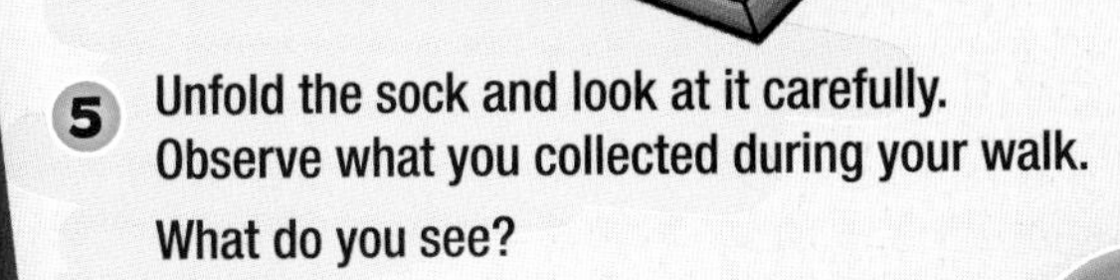

5. Unfold the sock and look at it carefully. Observe what you collected during your walk. What do you see?

THE SCIENCE BEHIND IT!

You may have collected seeds, burrs, grass, or twigs on your walk. Plants cannot move; they are stuck in the ground. Because of this, many plants have seeds that are light or sticky. Can you think of animals that have fur that is fuzzy like your sock? Plants use these animals to transport their seeds to new locations in the wild. The seeds stick to an animal in one place and then fall off in another. We already know that animals need plants to survive; animals eat plants and use their energy. But in this experiment, the data you collected shows that plants need animals, too!

FOOD CHAINS

Eat or Be Eaten

This owl might eat a mouse, another animal in the chain.

All the living things in an ecosystem are connected. If you are an animal in the wild, you have to stay alert. You need to eat food to stay alive. You need to watch out and not become a meal for an animal yourself.

JUST A LINK IN THE CHAIN

A **food chain** shows how living things get food and the energy they need to live. Some animals eat plants. Some animals eat other animals. For example, the Sun feeds grass, the grass feeds deer, and the deer feeds a wolf. Each link in this chain is food for the next link. The links show how each animal gets the energy it needs to survive.

IT ALL STARTS WITH THE SUN

The energy in most ecosystems starts with the Sun. Plants use the Sun's energy to make their own food. Animals then eat the plants. When the animal eats the plant, the energy goes from the plant to the animal. Plants are called **producers** because they make, or produce, their own food. Animals are called **consumers** because they consume plants and other animals to get the energy they need to survive. A healthy **food chain** needs producers and consumers. That's why it's eat or be eaten!

Most life depends on sunlight.

A Web of Life

How are plants and animals connected? Show some of the relationships in a food web.

1. Make a list of 5-10 different plants and animals in an ecosystem. For example, choose a forest, prairie, pond, or beach.

   Make a list of what each animal eats. For example, squirrels in the forest eat nuts from plants. Owls eat squirrels.

2. Cut cards from the pieces of construction paper. Write the plants from your list on green cards. Write the animals that eat plants on yellow cards. Write the animals that eat other animals on red cards. Write anything remaining on your list on blue cards.

3. Arrange the pieces in the order of what they eat. In the example, the owl would be at the top. The squirrel would be under the owl. The plant would be at the bottom.

4. Cut the yarn into 6-inch (15 cm) lengths and tape one piece of yarn to each pair of cards that link together.

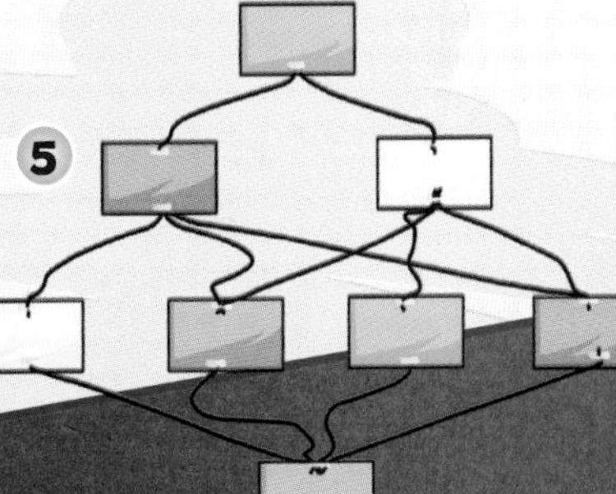

5. Can you see how the plants and animals link together? Are some animals or plants linked to more than one card?

Meat Eaters

Many animals eat plants for food, right? But did you know some plants eat animals for food? The Venus flytrap, for example, feeds on flies and other insects. These are special carnivorous plants that grow only in certain places on Earth. A carnivorous plant usually attracts its prey using a scent. When the insect lands, it's trapped and becomes food.

THE SCIENCE BEHIND IT!

A food web shows how plants and animals living in a community feed off one another. Each card may be linked to one or more other cards. All living things need energy, which they get from the food they eat. In a forest, for example, a tree gets its energy to grow from the Sun. Small animals, like squirrels, get their energy by eating the nuts from the tree, and the owls that live in the forest get their energy by eating squirrels. Everything is connected!

ADAPTATIONS

How Do They Survive?

You already know that certain plants live in certain places. Plants have **adaptations** that help them survive. Adaptations are changes in living things that help them live in their environment.

Cactus plants survive with little water.

Some trees change with the seasons.

DESERT ADAPTATIONS

Some deserts are hotter than others, but all deserts are dry. Plants need water, so how can they survive in the desert?

- Some store water in their stems or leaves.
- Many desert plants grow very slowly, which allows them to grow with less energy.
- Many desert plants have long roots that spread out or go deep into the ground to get water.

FOREST ADAPTATIONS

A temperate deciduous forest has four seasons: spring, summer, autumn, and winter. How have plants adapted to live there?

- Some trees have thick bark to protect them against cold winters.
- Wildflowers grow in the spring before trees overhead get leafy and block out the sunlight.

Keeping It Cool

How can some plants survive in very hot places with little water? This experiment may help you find out.

You will need:

- large clay flowerpot (cover the bottom hole with cardboard)
- lid to cover large flowerpot (a dinner plate will work)
- medium clay flowerpot that will fit inside large one
- small bag of sand
- 2 thermometers that will fit in the smaller pot
- water

1. Cover the bottom of the large flowerpot with a layer of sand 1/2 inch (1 cm) thick. Add water to the sand until it feels damp.

2. Place the medium flowerpot inside the larger pot. Fill in the space between the two pots with sand. Add water to the sand until it feels damp.

3. Place one thermometer inside the medium pot and cover the pots with the lid.

4. After two minutes, remove the lid and record the temperature inside the pot.

5. Place the thermometer back in the pot, replace the lid, and place the pots in a dry, sunny place. Place the second thermometer beside the pots and record the temperature outside the pot.

6. Record the temperature inside and outside the pots after 10, 20, and 30 minutes.

Record the temperature every day for several days, and make notes about the weather conditions and the dampness of the sand.

Ocean Plants

Many parts of the ocean don't have plants with roots. Sunlight can't reach far down into the water, so there is no light for photosynthesis. There are plants in the ocean, though. Phytoplankton (pheye toh PLANK tuhn) is a tiny plant that drifts throughout the surface waters of the ocean.

THE SCIENCE BEHIND IT!

The pots are made of porous clay. Air can move through the walls of the pots into the layer of sand between the pots. This allows the water in the sand to evaporate. Water uses the heat in its surroundings to evaporate. This removes heat from the inside of the pot which keeps it cool, allowing a plant to survive in a hot climate. This is also how you cool off when you sweat.

How Can We Care for OUR EARTH?

Caring for Earth is a huge job. It involves thinking about resources, taking care of plants and animals, recycling, and more.

RECYCLING

Recycling is the process of taking a product at the end of its useful life and then using all or part of it to make something else. When we **recycle**, we reduce the amount of waste sent to landfills. Many of us recycle paper, plastic, and glass. Did you know that we can also recycle a lot of electronics and things like batteries? What about recycling something that you can no longer use, like your old eyeglasses or cell phones?

At one time, wolves were nearly extinct.

Meet John Muir

Some call John Muir "the father of national parks." In 1892, he and attorney Warren Olney founded the Sierra Club, the first group dedicated to preserving nature. Muir said, "When we try to pick out anything by itself, we find it hitched to everything in the universe."

These are the founders of the Sierra Club: John Muir (l) and Warren Olney (r).

SAVING OUR ANIMALS

What is an **endangered** species? An **endangered species** is a species, or type, of animal native to an area that faces the possibility of dying out in the near future. In the United States, endangered species are protected by law. You cannot, for example, hunt an endangered animal or pick an endangered plant. Species may be endangered because of several reasons, such as **habitat** destruction or a change in climate. What can you do to protect endangered species?

Paper Beads

Does jewelry seem like science? This project shows that recycling is not only good for the Earth, it also can be fun!

You will need:

- bright-colored paper from magazines, gift-wrap, or catalogues
- button
- white glue or glue stick
- scissors
- string, yarn or fishing line

1. Cut strips of paper 1 inch (2.5 cm) wide and 4 inches (8 cm) long to make beads. Cut as many strips as you want beads.

2. Spread glue over half of the strip.

3. Roll the strip at the unglued end so that a hole is left in the center. This hole should be big enough to fit your string or fishing line. Continue rolling until the strip forms a bead. String the bead.

4. Once your beaded string is longer than 14 inches (36 cm) cut 3 more strips of paper 1 inch (2.5 cm) wide and 8 inches (20 cm) long and roll them to make large beads.

5. Tie the end of the string to the button.

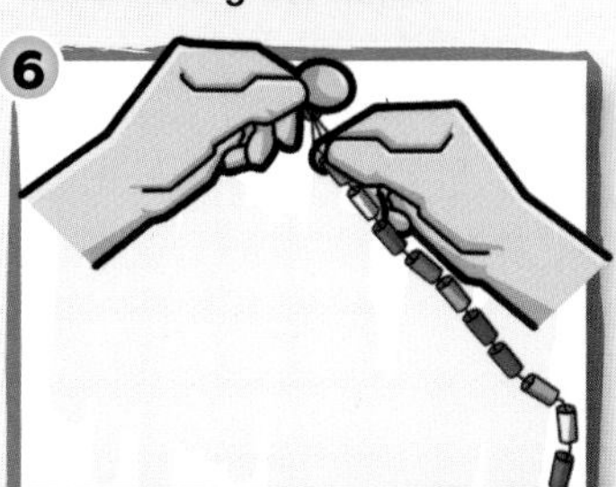

6. String the three large beads together at the other end and loop them to form a triangle shape. Tie the string to keep this shape.

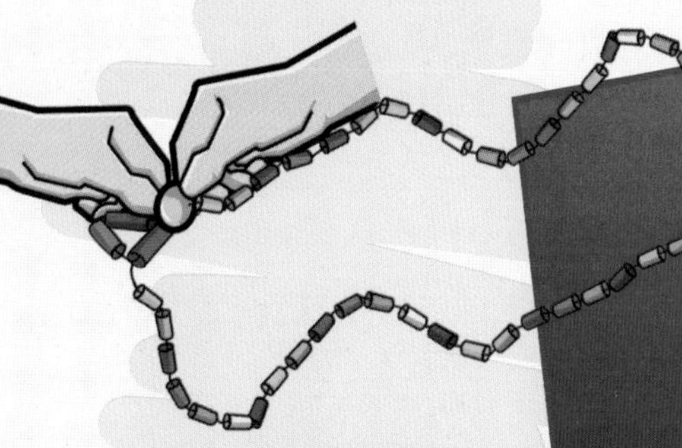

7. Slip the button through this triangle to wear your beaded string as a necklace.

THE SCIENCE BEHIND IT!

You just performed an act of recycling. Old magazines and papers can get a second life when we are creative. The act of gluing strips of paper into rolled beads can produce a beautiful work of art instead of adding more waste to landfills. Use your creativity to recycle.

SHOW WHAT YOU KNOW

Schools, libraries, and clubs sometimes have science fairs. What exactly is a science fair? How do you make a project for a science fair?

Ask Questions

A science fair is a way for you to use the same steps that scientists use to research a scientific topic. It starts with a question, like: How do different sediments layer to form rocks? How does the type of soil affect plant growth? How does the air pressure in a tire affect the way that a bicycle rolls? Does a truss make a bridge stronger? Which cleaning product kills the most bacteria? Once you have a question, it's time to figure out the answer.

Ask a question about something in science.

Research

Do some background research. Why should you research first and just not begin work? You might find some great information to help you better understand your question and how to answer it. Research will help you make a strong prediction. The research is also important because when you put your science fair project together, you'll be able to show the groundwork that you did first. If your project is in a contest, your research will impress the judges!

Research to find out more.

State a Hypothesis

What hypothesis can you make about the plant in the Sun?

Create a hypothesis. A hypothesis is a prediction about how something works. Your hypothesis needs to be something you can test. Your hypothesis might be something like, "If I keep one plant in a closet and one on a sunny windowsill, the plant on the windowsill will grow faster." It's important in your experiment to only have one variable. In the hypothesis about plants, the variable is where the plant is placed—either on the windowsill or in the closet. It's important that the plants are the same in every other way. They should have the same soil, the same amount of food and water, and start at the same height.

Measurements are one way to make observations.

Observe

Plan your experiment to test your hypothesis. You should do your experiment more than one time to be sure that the results are the same each time. Take careful measurements. Use your senses, observe, use tools to measure—and record your results.

Analyze

Analyze your data. Did you get the results you expected? What did you find out? Summarize your data and draw conclusions about it.

What do your observations indicate?

WRITE A REPORT

YOUR REPORT SHOULD INCLUDE:

1. a title page
2. an overview of what you did
3. your hypothesis
4. a summary of the research you did
5. a list of materials you used
6. the procedure for your experiment
7. your data
8. your conclusion
9. a list of the resources you used

MAKE A DISPLAY

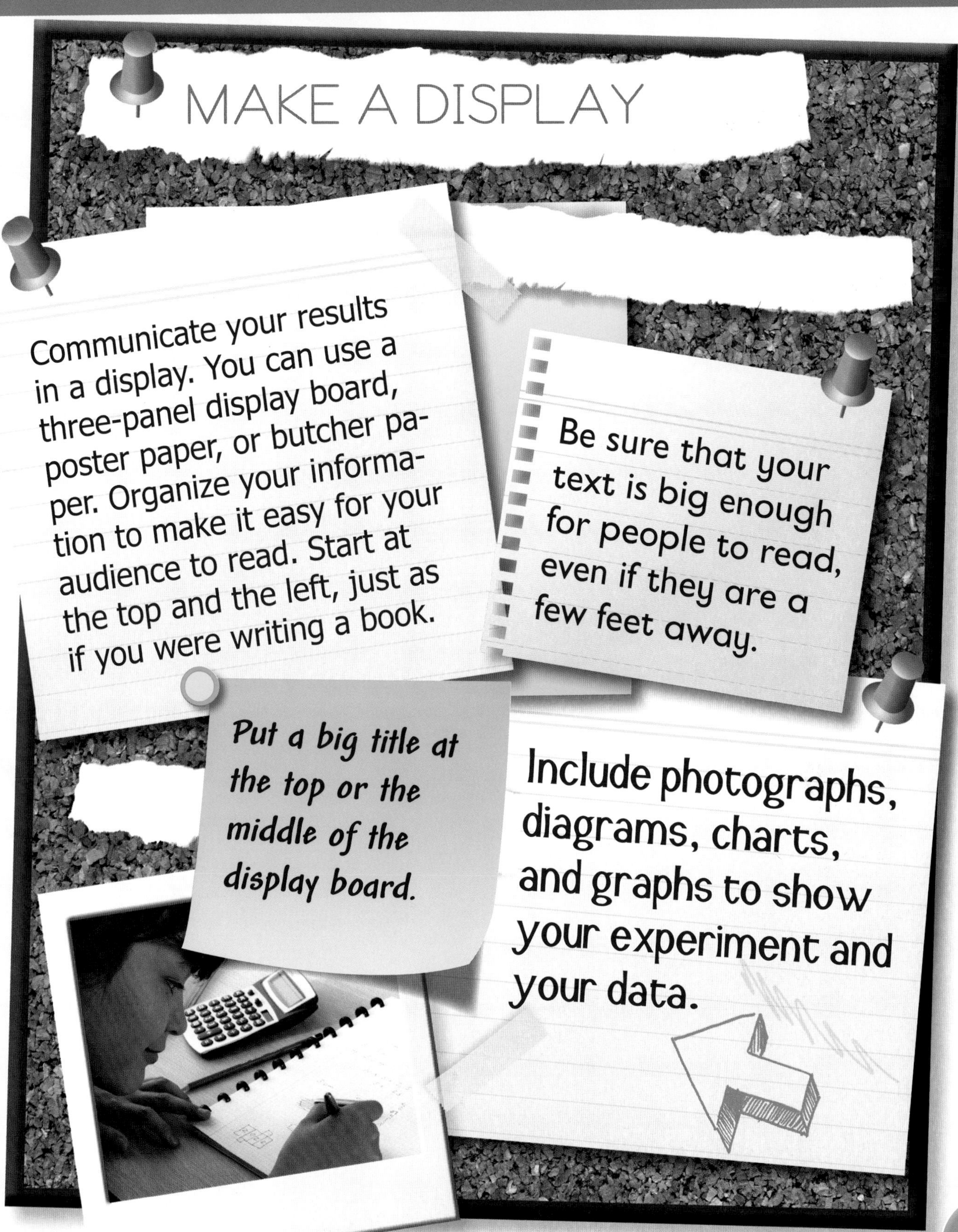

Communicate your results in a display. You can use a three-panel display board, poster paper, or butcher paper. Organize your information to make it easy for your audience to read. Start at the top and the left, just as if you were writing a book.

Be sure that your text is big enough for people to read, even if they are a few feet away.

Put a big title at the top or the middle of the display board.

Include photographs, diagrams, charts, and graphs to show your experiment and your data.

GLOSSARY

abyssal plain (uh-BIS-uhl PLAYN) the broad, flat floor of the deep ocean

acid (AS-id) a substance that has a pH value of less than 7

adaptation (ad-ap-TAY-shun) a trait of a plant or an animal that helps it survive in a certain place

air pressure (AYR PRESH-ur) the force of air, pushing on any surface in contact with it

amber (AM-bur) fossilized tree sap or resin

aquatic (uh-KWOT-ik) living or growing in water

arc (AHRK) a curved or semicircular line

asthma (AZ-muh) a lung disorder with symptoms including coughing, a tight chest, and difficulty breathing

atmosphere (AT-muhs-feer) 1. the envelope of gasses around the Earth; 2. a unit of measurement of water pressure

atom (AT-uhm) the smallest part of an element

attract (uh-TRAKT) to draw objects near

axis (AK-sis) an imaginary line around which an object spins

base (BAYS) a substance that has a pH greater than 7

biome (BYE-ohm) a region with a certain climate, plants, and animals, such as a desert

brain (BRAYN) control center of the nervous system

canyon (KAN-yuhn) a deep narrow valley with steep sides

cardiovasculatory system (car-dee-oh-VAS-kyu-luh-tor-ee SIS-tuhm) the body system that moves blood throughout the body

carnivorous (kahr-NIV-ur-uhs) meat-eating

cave (CAVE) a large naturally hollowed-out place underground or in rock above ground

cell (SEL) the smallest unit in a living organism

chemical reaction (KEM-i-kuhl ree-AK-shuhn) when two or more substances interact to form a different substance

cirque (SURK) a bowl-shaped hollow with steep walls formed by erosion from a glacier

classify (KLAS-uh-fye) to place into a category or group

climate (KLYE-muht) weather conditions in one place over a long period or time

cloud (KLOWD) a collection of water droplets hanging in the air

cochlea (KOK-lee-uh) a spiral-shaped structure in the middle ear

compressed (kuhm-PREST) pressed together in a space smaller than normal

conduction (kuhn-DUK-shuhn) heat transfer between two objects that are touching each other

conductor (kuhn-DUK-tur) a substance that transfers energy from one place to another

cone (CONE) cells in the retina of the eye that help us see color and brightness

consumer (kuhn-SOO-mur) an organism that feeds on plants or other animals

continental shelf (kon-tuh-NEN-tuhl SHELF) the edges of a continent under shallow sea water

control (kuhn-TROHL) part of an experiment that stays the same to show the effects of something that is changed

convection (kuhn-VEK-shuhn) transfer of heat caused by the movement of liquid or gas

cyclone (SYE-klone) a storm with heavy rain and winds that rotates over the sea

defect (DEE-fekt) something that is wrong

diaphragm (DYE-uh-fram) main muscle that controls breathing

digestive system (di-JES-tiv SIS-tuhm) system of organs that turn food into nutrients the body can use and rid the body of waste

dormant (DOR-muhnt) in a state where growth or development slows down or stops

drought (DROWT) a long period without rainfall

ecosystem (EE-koh-sis-tuhm) a system formed by living organisms and their environment

electron (e-LEK-tron) a negatively charged particle in an atom

element (EL-uh-muhnt) a substance that cannot be broken down into simpler substances

endangered species (en-DAYN-jurd SPEE-sees) a species of animal or plant in danger of becoming extinct

entomologist (en-tuh-MOL-uh-jist) a scientist who studies insects

enzyme (EN-zime) a protein that can increase the rate of a chemical reaction

equator (i-KWAY-tur) imaginary line around the Earth, half way between the North and South Poles

erosion (i-ROH-zhuhn) wearing away by the action of water, glaciers, wind, waves, and so on

esophagus (i-SOF-uh-guhs) the passage where food moves between the throat and stomach

evidence (EV-i-duhns) information that tends to support or disprove something

fault line (FAWLT LINE) a break in Earth's crust

flower (FLOW-ur) reproductive organ of fruit-bearing plants

food chain (FOOD CHAYN) a group of living things, each of which feeds on others

force (FOHRS) a push or a pull

fossil (FOS-uhl) the preserved remains, impression, or trace of a living thing

freezing point (FREE-zing POYNT) the temperature at which liquid changes to solid

friction (FRIK-shuhn) force that opposes motion between two touching surfaces

front (FRUHNT) where two air masses meet

fulcrum (FUHL-kruhm) the support on which a lever lifts

gas (GAS) a substance that is neither solid nor liquid and expands to fill a space

geologist (jee-OL-uh-jist) a scientist who studies Earth's structure

geothermal energy (jee-oh-THUR-muhl EN-ur-jee) energy produced from the heat inside the Earth

geyser (GYE-zur) a hot spring that sends jets of water and steam into the air

glacier (GLAY-shur) a large body of ice and snow that moves slowly under its own weight

global warming (GLOH-buhl WAWRM-ing) an increase in the average temperature of the Earth

Great Plains (GRAYT PLAYNZ) a mostly level region east of the Rocky Mountains in the U.S.

greenhouse gas (GREEN-hows GAS) a gas that reflects radiation from the surface of the Earth

habitat (HAB-i-tat) a place where a plant and/or an animal lives

heat (HEET) energy that is created when molecules move

hurricane (HUR-i-kane) a severe tropical storm with rain and winds above 74 miles (119 km) per hour

hypothesis (hye-POTH-uh-sis) a testable prediction about how a scientific experiment will turn out

igneous (IG-nee-uhs) rock formed when magma or lava cools and hardens

infer (in-FUR) to draw a conclusion from data

infrared radiation (in-fruh-RED ray-dee-AY-shuhn) electromagnetic radiation with wavelengths longer than visible light rays

invertebrate (in-VUR-tuh-brit) a creature that does not have a backbone

large intestine (LAHRJ IN-TES-tin) the wider part of the intestine in which water is absorbed out of undigested food

law (LAW) a statement describing a natural phenomenon that always occurs under certain conditions

lightning (LITE-ning) flashes of light caused by a discharge of electricity in clouds or between clouds and the Earth

light-year (LITE-YEER) how far light travels in a year (approximately 5.87 trillion miles/9.46 trillion km)

liquid (LIK-wid) a state of matter that can change shape but not volume

longitudinal wave (lon-ji-TOOD-i-nuhl WAVE) a wave, such as a sound wave, in which the particles in the wave move in the same direction as the wave itself

machine (muh-SHEEN) a device that does work

magma (MAG-muh) molten rock deep below the surface of the Earth

magnet (MAG-nit) a piece of metal that has the power to attract iron or steel

magnetic field (mag-NET-ik FEELD) the space around a magnet that has magnetic force

malleable (MAL-ee-uh-buhl) able to be shaped or bent without breaking

matter (MA-tur) the substance any object is made of

measure (MEZH-ur) to determine the area, size, volume, weight, or dimension of something

medium (MEE-dee-uhm) a substance through which something is carried or transferred

metal (MET-uhl) a class of elements including gold and copper that conduct heat and electricity

Mohs scale (MOHS SKALE) a scale that measures the hardness of minerals

motor nerve (MOH-ur NERV) a nerve that conveys messages to muscles

nerve (NERV) a tissue that sends messages between the brain and the body's organs

nervous system (NERV-uhs SIS-tuhm) the organ system that includes the brain and nerves

neutral (NOO-truhl) a substance that is neither an acid nor a base

neutron (NOO-tron) a neutral particle that has no electrical charge

nucleus (NOO-klee-uhs) the central body of a cell

orbit (OR-bit) the path in which one object travels around another

paleontologist (pay-lee-uhn-TOL-uh-jist) a scientist who studies the fossil record of Earth

Pangaea (pan-JEE-uh) the landmass that existed when all continents on Earth were joined, from about 300 to 200 million years ago

Periodic table (peer-ee-OD-ik TAY-buhl) a table that shows the elements arranged in the order of their atomic numbers

pH (PEE AYCH) a number that expresses whether a solution is an acid or a base; a pH of 7 is neutral

phase change (FAZE CHAYNJ) a change from one state (solid or liquid or gas) to another, such as liquid to gas

photosynthesis (foh-toh-SIN-thuh-sis) the process a plant uses to makes food

physical change (FIZ-i-kuhl CHAYNJ) a change that affects a physical property, but not a chemical property, of a substance

plasma (PLAZ-muh) a state of matter of a highly energized substance

plate (PLATE) one large section of the Earth's crust

plate tectonics (PLATE tek-TON-iks) the movement of Earth's plates

precipitation (pree-sip-i-TAY-shuhn) rain, snow, or hail

predator (PRED-uh-tur) an animal that hunts other animals for food

prehistoric (pree-his-TOR-ik) related to a period of time before history was recorded

prey (PRAY) an animal eaten by other animals

producer (proh-DOO-sur) a plant's role of creating food in food chain or food web

projectile (pruh-JEK-tile) an object pushed or forced to move

proton (PROH-ton) a stable particle in the nucleus of an atom

radiation (ray-dee-AY-shunn) the process in which an atom gives off particles or energy

recycle (ree-SYE-kuhl) reuse rather than throw away

reflex action (REE-fleks AK-shuhn) an action that occurs when the nervous system reacts to a stimulus

refraction (ree-FRAK-shuhn) the change in the direction of a wave when it goes from one medium to another

repel (ri-PEL) to force or push something away

reproduce (ree-pruh-DOOS) to create offspring

root (ROOT) the part of the plant that anchors the plant and absorbs water and nutrients from the ground

scientific method (sye-uhn-TIF-ik METH-uhd) an organized way of finding something out

sedimentary (sed-i-MEN-tuh-ree) rock formed when eroded rocks are pressed together

sediment (SED-i-muhnt) a material that comes from eroded rocks

sense (SENS) how organisms get information about the world: sight, sound, taste, touch, smell

sensor (SENS-ur) an organ that detects and responds to a stimulus like light or heat

sensory nerve (SENS-uh-ree NURV) a nerve that experiences a stimulus

small intestine (SMAWL in-TES-tin) the upper part of the intestine where food is digested

solar energy (SOH-lur EN-ur-jee) energy from the Sun

solar system (SOH-lur SIS-tuhm) the group of planets that orbit around a star or sun

solid (SOL-id) the state of matter that retains its shape and size

spectrum (SPEK-truhm) the colored light waves that form when light goes through a prism

spinal cord (SPINE-uhl KORD) a thick cord of nerve tissue from the brain through the spinal column

stalactite (stuh-LAK-tite) mineral deposit that forms on a cave's ceiling

stalagmite (stuh-LAG-mite) mineral deposit that forms on a cave's floor

state (STATE) the physical condition of matter: gas, liquid, solid, or plasma

static electricity (STAT-ik i-lek-TRIS-i-tee) electricity that builds up on an object, such as a thundercloud

stem (STEM) the stalk that supports a leaf, flower, or fruit

stomach (STUHM-uhk) an organ that stores and digests food

stomata (STOH-muh-tuh) openings in a plant where gases like water vapor move in and out of the plant

storm surge (STORM SURJ) the rise in sea level along a coast that is caused by a severe storm at sea

submersible (sub-MUR-suh-buhl) a craft able to operate under water

tendon (TEN-duhn) a tissue connecting muscle to bone

theory (THEE-uh-ree) a rule, idea, or principle that explains a phenomenon

thermal energy (THUR-muhl EN-ur-jee) energy created when particles move

tide (TIDE) the variation in the ocean's surface level

tissue (TISH-oo) cells combined to form structures, such as muscle

tornado (tor-NAY-doh) a destructive funnel-shaped column of air that passes over land

trajectory (truh-JEC-tuh-ree) the curved path of a projectile

transpiration (tran-spuh-RAY-shuhn) the loss of water in a plant through evaporation

transverse wave (TRANZ-vurs WAVE) a wave that moves in two directions

tropics (TROP-iks) the region of the Earth's surface near the equator

tsunami (soo-NAH-mee) a large sea wave that is made by a seaquake or a volcanic eruption under the sea

typhoon (tye-FOON) tropical cyclone occurring in the western Pacific or Indian oceans

vacuum (VAK-yoom) a space completely free of matter or air

vertebrate (VUR-tuh-brit) an animal that has a backbone or spine

villi (VIL-eye) body parts that absorb nutrients in the digestive system

volcano (vol-KAY-noh) an opening in the crust of the Earth that ejects molten, gaseous and solid material

vortex (VOR-teks) a spinning mass of air or water

wave (WAVE) a ripple that moves through a medium to transfer energy from one point to another

white noise (WITE NOYZ) a noise that is made by combining all the frequencies that can be heard

FIND IT!

References for Reading and Research

Janice VanCleave's Guide to More of the Best Science Fair Projects. Janice VanCleave. John Wiley & Sons, Inc. (2000). This book includes exciting and easy-to-understand science projects.

The Everything Kids' Science Experiments Book. Tom Robinson. Adams Media (2001). Fun facts and amazing projects are waiting for you in the pages of this book!

Save the Earth Science Experiments: Science Fair Projects for Eco-Kids. Elizabeth Snoke Harris. Lark Books (2009). Want to experiment with science and learn more about preserving our precious Earth, all at the same time? Check out this book full of eco-friendly projects.

Earth. Susanna van Rose. DK Children (2005). This book gives an overview of Earth science topics from rocks and glaciers to climate and volcanoes.

Zap! Blink! Taste! Think! Exciting Life Science for Curious Minds. Janet Parks Chahour. Barron's Educational Series (2003). From botany to forensics, this book covers a wide range of life science topics.

Want to find out more about volcanoes? Check out this site.
http://volcano.oregonstate.edu/

Visit Time for Kids to find out the latest science news.
www.timeforkids.com/TFK/

NASA's website has information about land, air, water, and weather.
http://kids.mtpe.hq.nasa.gov/

The National Weather Service website is a great place to find out about storms from hurricanes to blizzards.
www.nws.noaa.gov/om/reachout/kidspage.shtml

National Geographic for Kids showcases information about science from animals to the galaxies.
http://kids.nationalgeographic.com/

Visit NOVA's website to delve deeply into science.
www.pbs.org/wgbh/nova/

The Exploratorium features all sorts of science experiments you can do at home.
www.exploratorium.edu/science_explorer/index.html

INDEX